SEVEN BRIEF LESSONS
ON **MAGIC**

SEVEN BRIEF LESSONS
ON MAGIC

Paul Tyson

CASCADE *Books* • Eugene, Oregon

SEVEN BRIEF LESSONS ON MAGIC

Cascade Books
An Imprint of Wipf and Stock Publishers
199 W. 8th Ave., Suite 3
Eugene, OR 97401

www.wipfandstock.com

PAPERBACK ISBN: 978-1-5326-9041-9
HARDCOVER ISBN: 978-1-5326-9042-6
EBOOK ISBN: 978-1-5326-9043-3

Cataloguing-in-Publication data:

Names: Tyson, Paul G., author.

Title: Seven brief lessons on magic / Paul Tyson.

Description: Eugene, OR: Cascade Books, 2019 | Includes bibliographical references.

Identifiers: ISBN 978-1-5326-9041-9 (paperback) | ISBN 978-1-5326-9042-6 (hardcover) | ISBN 978-1-5326-9043-3 (ebook)

Subjects: LCSH: Magic | Metaphysics | Materialism | Religion and culture | Christianity—Philosophy | Platonists | Secularism | Religion and science

Classification: BT40 T97 2019 (paperback) | BT40 (ebook)

Manufactured in the U.S.A.   04/18/19

CONTENTS

WHY DOES MAGIC MATTER?

MAGIC AND SCIENCE

This book is about the reality of magic in an age of science. It is about what the truth lens of science can see and what it cannot see. It is also about non-scientific truths.

Thankfully, science can see many things very clearly. For example, science can see how infections in our bodies work, and what can be done to stop them. This has eliminated many common causes of death. Three cheers for science! But while science can see and manipulate some very important aspects of reality, it remains remarkably blind to other things.

Science can see hormones, conditioned social behaviors, and biological necessities, but science cannot see love. Does this mean that (really) love is only what science can see, and the magic of love is just made up? I am sure hormones and so forth have a great deal to do with the human experience of love. But what about our sense of the intrinsic and transcendent meaning of love; is that just an imagined and subjective gloss on the objective biological facts? Is love *real* in magical, non-scientific terms, or can we only speak of reality itself in scientific terms? Another way of putting this question is to ask, are all poets liars?

It seems to me that, obviously, all poets are not liars. Poets imaginatively articulate things that, in some manner, are really there. There is a truth to love that is a magical truth, a truth beyond the ken of science. Indeed, love is but one example of an obvious magical feature of our daily lives that science cannot see. Thought is another example.

We know a great deal about the brain, we can simulate human intelligence to a remarkable degree, and computerized chess programs can beat grandmasters. We are even fiddling around with so-called quantum computing, trying to escape linear information processing in ways that may end up making computers more like our own brains. Yet, try as we might, we just can't "see" a thought or the conscious mind with science. Is this because *really* there are no thoughts or minds, there are only brains and the bio-electrical processing of sensory stimuli? Once we have a perfect simulation of how our brains work, will we have thoughts and minds? Is Apple's Siri actually talking with us? Or, is there a magical *more* to thought, communication, and consciousness that our science just can't see?

What about beauty?

I could go on: friendship, justice, dignity, hope, purpose, joy, despair, truth, evil, goodness . . . . All of these obvious, everyday features of our experience of *the meaning of reality* are to some degree visible to the gaze of science, and yet that which is most humanly significant about these things remains stubbornly invisible to science.

We can sharpen the question of what makes something invisible to science by asking what *is* visible to science.

Science studies **m**easurable, **m**aterial, and **m**athematically **m**odelable reality: 4M reality. This reality really does exist. But is this the *only* face of reality? What do we make of all those obvious qualities and meanings that we directly experience in our everyday lives that an exclusively 4M vision of reality cannot see? Let us call anything that 4M reality cannot see, magic. Then let us ask, is magic real? And if it is, what is magic's relation to the reality that science shows us?

These questions are far from academic. What we think about values and meanings, and whether we think they are real and at least potentially true or not, deeply affects the manner in which we actually live. If we are modern realists and make decisions on the basis that really only material things and manipulative powers exist, then we will not take values and meanings very seriously. A realist politician, for example, will be quite happy to use statistically visible things—like a common belief in intrinsic human dignity—as a power tool that can have good manipulative leverage on public opinion and electoral outcomes. But such realism has no understanding of the actual realty of intrinsic human dignity itself. This sort of measurable realism reduces all values and meanings to instrumentally useful opinions and—so I will argue—greatly impoverishes our view of reality and de-humanizes our actions.

Reductive realism seems sensible to us because of a complex feature of the modern world that sociologists call disenchantment. The fact is, in many ways we have come to think that magical meanings and higher purposes are no longer part of practical reality or academic knowledge. This means we tend to think about truth and power in ways that ignore magic, even if magic is obvious in our actual lives. This is causing us some very serious problems.

Recent centuries have seen the rise of de-magicing ways of understanding and manipulating nature, tied in with the rise of modern science. This has gone together with new technologies, the industrial revolution, the information revolution, the financial revolution, and so on. With the aid of modern science we have generated a new and functionally de-magical global environment of human meaning and power. We now have astonishing power over nature. But this power comes at a price. We have cut qualitative and spiritual wisdom off from knowledge and power. With our wisdom-divorced power, we have developed a voracious energy and resource consuming way of life that seems to heed no natural limits . . . this could end very badly.

How we understand the meaning and value of nature in an age of science, when meaning and value themselves seem beyond the scope of truth, has become a very serious problem for us. Perhaps we should try and re-think how we understand nature? Perhaps we should see if we can find ways of thinking about the truth, the reality, and the importance of all those magical meanings and values that we actually cherish? To do this, we would need a different approach to magic.

AN OVERVIEW OF THESE SEVEN BRIEF LESSONS ON MAGIC

In this short book, I hope to persuade you that there is more than one way of thinking about magic. In fact, I am going to present you with four theories about magic: the very old **animist theory of magic**, where Nature herself is thought of as divine and living; the classical and medieval **Platonist theory of magic**, where nature is saturated in transcendent meaning from beyond herself; the modern **supernatural theory of magic**, where nature is not magical, but a separated supernatural reality is magical; the modern **anti-magical theory**, where magic is thought of as, simply put, unreal. I hope to show you that each of these theories has its strengths and weaknesses, and—surprisingly—each of these theories has its impacts on how we actually *experience* the world we live in today.

The seven lessons on magic that I will spin you through follow this outline:

The first lesson points out some of the fascinating ways in which we now live in a high age of magic. There are many contradictions and dissonances in this way of life, but to sociologists such dissonances are particularly interesting windows that give us a very helpful view on what makes any distinctive cultural lifeworld work. This lesson is particularly interested in the dissonance between, on the one hand, a reductively factual and instrumental approach to knowledge and, on the other, an imaginative and internalized meaning culture that is addicted to magical fantasies. For the distinctive shape of this dissonance shows us that our dominant and modern theories of magic—the supernatural and anti-magical theories—are seriously failing the modern world. The question that guides the next six lessons, then, is whether we can find some way to recover and rework either the animist or Platonist theories of magic, and integrate a more viable theory of magic with our science.

This second lesson introduces the four basic theories of magic to be discussed. It also seeks to briefly indicate why a persistent disjuncture between the knowledge-and-power axis of practical action and the value-and-meaning axis of personal significance is a function of how our modern theories of magic view reality.

The third and fourth lessons briefly explore disenchantment. Disenchantment refers to the way we modern people reflexively experience the world as *un*magical. It is important to understand that in very significant ways, disenchantment really did happened to the life-world of modernity. We will look at that in lesson three. But that is only half of the story. In other regards, disenchantment definitely did not happen. We will look at that in lesson four. These two lessons are mainly concerned with understanding how the two modern theories of magic—the supernatural and anti-magical theories—have both succeeded and failed in shaping the life-world of the modern scientific age.

The fifth lesson looks at the magic of quality and purpose. A quality—like beauty—is not something you can measure; it is a valuable meaning that engenders wonder and admiration. A purpose—like love—is something that gives our intentions a meaningful aim, and again, this is not physically measurable. To the anti-magical view, quality and purpose have no objective existence. When we look at ourselves from an anti-magical outlook, through the lens of modern science, then moral and aesthetic qualities and intrinsic and ultimate purposes only exist as subjective constructs of our consciousness, they are not actual features of objective reality. But this view of reality is very hard to believe. In this lesson we will explore how quality and purpose can, and should, be understood as real.

The sixth lesson explores questions of magic and essence. This is a lesson about the cosmic mystery of intelligibility. That our ideas and knowledge of the world can be more or less true is the most basic undergirding premise of modern science, and yet this is a premise that modern science (and modern philosophy) cannot establish. The argument in this lesson will seek to show that intelligibility is real and that our modern theories of magic are problematic.

The seventh and final lesson in this book is my attempt to persuade you that a reworked Platonist view of magic remains the best theory of magic currently on offer.

From the outset, it is worth considering one's own starting assumptions about magic. What do *you* think about the nature of our experience of meaning and value in the world? Do you think nature is itself magical, or is the wonder of the world only really an internal sensibility of our own consciousness? Or maybe rather than some hard either/or, perhaps there is a both/and relationship between knowledge and meaning? Do you think that nature is just composed of material objects and entirely physical laws, but that some supernatural realm produced this law-defined and intricately coherent natural world? Do you think that some divine Mind undergirds nature now such that value and meaning are—all at once—in our own minds, in nature, and beyond nature?

The most common response I get when I ask people what they think about magic is that it is just a bit of imaginative fun that has no real bearing on our lives. I understand this view well as I myself am all in favor of imaginative fun. But sociologically, both magic and make-believe are very serious things. If you too start from the imaginative fun view of magic, you may be in for a surprise when you read the first lesson.

WE LIVE IN A HIGH AGE OF MAGIC

Gandalf, Dumbledore, and Rincewind—to name-drop just a few of the most famous wizards of our times—are far better known to us than our real masters of power and illusion. Harry Potter is world famous, and any reader of Terry Pratchett will have quite a sophisticated theoretical knowledge of Disc World magic. In contrast, very few people know who the main players are in our own mysterious world of high financial alchemy. What actually makes the fabulous world of currency markets and derivative trading fly may as well be a genuine occult mystery to most people (many traders, bankers, treasury officials, and finance ministers included).

We live in an age where we are embedded in skillfully manufactured collective illusions and where our most familiar objects are astonishing technological devices with extraordinary powers, whose inner workings we hardly understand at all. But these devices are not simply wands and portals that give *us* power and knowledge, they are tools of power *to those who provide them to us*. Profiling algorithms and information collection are deeply integral to nearly every internet search and every social media interaction we undertake. We have grown accustomed to detailed and pervasive information gathering and intrusive surveillance technologies that both map and steer almost every aspect of our lives. We are like fish in a sea of translucent liquid power: power in the form of the skillful control and distribution of information, of pervasive data gathering, and of psychologically subtle collective choice influence. But we do not see this sea, for we are immersed in it—it is the very medium of our way of life.[1]

On the one hand, this is all a bit sinister. On the other hand, we love it. We are pretty well addicted to the dazzling seductions of our communication, information, and entertainment technologies: tools that obliterate the normal texture of space and time, that deeply re-fashion pre-social-media ways of relating to others, and that powerfully erode simply "being present" to where we physically are. These technologies refashion our imaginative landscape as well. They give free vent to the enjoyment, projection, and marketing of astonishing fantasies. A manufactured hyper-real world of wishful fantasy is now a mundane part of the way we communicate, relax, and do business. And yet, having been raised by the educational institutions of the modern scientific age, we largely accept the prevailing materialist motherhood truths about what reality is really like. Our educated truths about the real and public world exclude enchantment, deny reality to all spiritual beings and powers, and reject the very possibility that frameworks of transcendent truth structure the immanent contours of ordinary life.

Practically, we live in a world of technological magic. Wonder, illusion, and the harnessing of powers that we do not understand is the wallpaper of our daily lives. Intellectually, however, we adhere to a realism of reductive materialism. Such is the bizarre dissonance entailed in this fantasy-reality relationship that it can be stated the other way around and it is still true. We could say that magical technology now is our cold hard realism, and yet we still "doctrinally" believe in the fantasy realm of meaningless objective facts. Our day-to-day attitude towards the world is one of a flat, instrumental pragmatism, yet at the level of collective imagination, we like to watch movies, play computer games, and read books about enchanted worlds, gods, magical powers, and superhuman

1. See Bauman, *Liquid Modernity*; Zuboff, *Age of Surveillance Capitalism*.

beings. Further, we are deeply drawn to shared narratives with a tacitly transcendent horizon to the high and deep things of the human condition: love, purpose, courage, dignity, destiny, and cosmic meaning. And yet we are educated to know the difference between hard and practical facts, and subjective meanings and non-factual "beliefs."

To put it bluntly, the primary furnishings of our minds uphold an armed barrier between the way we think about the outer world of factual scientific knowledge and practical technological power and the inner world of imagination, meaning, purpose, and value. This barrier is very much tied up with how we use and understand modern science, and rests on the assumed validity of both the supernatural and the anti-magical theories of magic. (More about these modern theories of magic will follow in lesson two.) We are born into a divided cosmos defined by a de-magiced nature on one side and a fantastic or supernatural imaginative magic on the other side, and don't know anything different. The dissonance between the dry instrumental facts and the wild imaginative meanings native to our life-world seems like an entirely reasonable and realistic situation to us. We don't want imagination and meaning to win over our "realist" conception of knowledge and power, or the other way around. We are deeply habituated to navigate our lives of practical reality and constructed meaning using the carefully policed border crossings that keep these segregated zones apart. But actually . . . we are not really content with this situation.

We are voracious consumers of magical fantasy stories. We love nature, and sense its magic, and yet we isolate its aesthetic and spiritual value from its practical exploitation and financial significance in ways that may well prove catastrophic to both nature and our own flourishing. We know this is a problem, but we don't know how to fix it. We are callous pragmatists and romantic dreamers all at the same time. Our collective fantasies, our alternative health and wellbeing shopping habits, and some modern types of religion and spirituality simply can't get enough magic, and yet our academic knowledge culture has no idea what magic might be other than the immature superstitions of pre-scientific ignorance.

We can't stop dreaming about magic and cosmic meaning. Re-imagining the Middle Ages is the backdrop for so much of our popular magical fiction. That was a world full of symbolic mythic creatures, a world where wisdom and knowledge were integral, a world where higher knowledge was of essential natures and transcendent realities. To that lost world, the right spoken word had a commanding sympathy with the cosmic Word that ordered all of heaven and earth. But our world is not like that. Or so the sensible scientific realism of our modern academy seems to be telling us.

The *Encyclopedia Britannica* notes that A. J. Ayer's 1936 book *Language, Truth and Logic* was "one of the bestselling works of serious twentieth-century philosophy." This is a book of famously deflationary philosophy that defines everything as meaningless if it cannot pass muster under a rigorously empirical and logical reductionism. Leaving to one side the ironic fact that the truth claims of Ayer's own logical positivism did not pass this muster themselves, it needs to be pointed out that even a breakaway best seller in "serious twentieth-century philosophy" does not sell many books. I could not find it (or any other book of "serious philosophy") listed when searching around for bestselling books of the twentieth century. What I did find was fantasy writers: the "over 100 million copies sold" category was dominated by Tolkien, C. S. Lewis, and J. K. Rowling (over 500 million books have now been sold in her Harry Potter series). And when it comes to all-time best sellers, the Bible is estimated to have had around 5 billion copies sold and distributed to date. So, whatever our academy is telling us about knowledge and reason, fantasy and religion are far more interesting to people than "serious" modern philosophy is.

When you look at book sales, you might surmise that Tolkien, Lewis, and Rowling are far more important to us than the philosophers and theologians of our times. Clearly, our fantasy writers speak to us. Could it be that even our pragmatic consumer society has a deep hunger for visions of a meaningful cosmos, for high quests, for some living magical dimension to everyday reality? Could it be that fantasy scratches a basic human itch that our "serious philosophy" does not even seem to know about? Could it even be that magic has not actually left us? Might magic be planning an escape from behind the great wall that the modern divided cosmos has erected so as to contain it within merely subjective personal fantasy?

To sum this first lesson up, there are four quite distinct senses in which we, today, do indeed live in a high age of magic.

Firstly, *magic is what causes us to delight in and intellectually explore the world, in a state of wonder.* This is, I think, a perennial feature of the human condition. Beauty, love, goodness, truth: every time we experience these qualitative encounters with others and the world, we taste a quality of life, of experience, and of thought that is magical. As this cannot be obliterated from the experience of being human: all ages must be ages of magic.

Secondly, *magic is inextricably located within our socially experienced, meaningful view of reality.* This is interesting. Sociologists of knowledge understand that all human conceptions of reality are socially constructed.[2] This does not mean that there is no such thing as reality existing independently of socially situated and practiced visions of reality, it only means that the only visions of reality that *we* ever have are socially situated. This is—according to thinkers like Johann Georg Hamann—a deeply magical feature of the human experience of meaning. I make sense of the world through the language, idioms, education, relationships, imaginative landscapes, practices, narratives, histories, hopes and fears of the social world into which I am born.[3] Meaning itself is this richly contextual and deeply human feature of our experience of the world. Yet it is not only the human world that shapes our meaning, the natural world's interaction with the human world equally shapes our meanings and our understanding of reality. There is a creative partnership between human interpretation and the meaningful world that is amazing, indeed magical. Even so, we modern people don't tend to *think* about our conception of reality as magical. If we think about it at all, we tend to think of a *realistic* understanding of nature as the *exact*

2. See Berger and Luckmann, *The Social Construction of Reality.*

3. See Hamann, "Metacritique of the Purism of Reason" in Haynes (ed.), *Hamann*, 205–18.

opposite of the magical. But, for reasons we shall unpack as we go, that assumption is a cultural blind spot. That we have a meaningful understanding of reality itself is, inescapably, magical, and this reality is intrinsically in a state of unfolding and ongoing imaginative play. In a decidedly cheeky way, this is what that brilliant and irritating postmodernist Jacques Derrida pointed out. For actually, a reductive scientistic anti-magical view of reality is magical to the extent that it projects a meaning (of no meaning) onto reality. Ironically, even the anti-magical vision of starkly factual realism is an enchanted story of meaning.

Thirdly—though this gives the term "magic" a meaning that I am not really comfortable with—*magic has a social meaning connected with power in a manner that is usually contrasted with "religion."* Here, at least schematically, religion entails submission of one's life to a higher power, but magic entails the manipulation of the minds and lives of others for one's own ends. Without getting into interesting arguments about whether or how you can differentiate magic from religion (or, in this "power" sense, science), clearly a magician is a figure of power. Further, the magician's instrumental powers comes from arcane yet fundamental knowledge. If one sort of magic is the magician's casting of illusions and the use of subtle power to manipulate and control both nature and the lives of others, then our age of commercially and governmentally applied information and communication technologies situates us squarely within a very sophisticated age of magic. But obviously we live in an age of good magic as well. The positive wonders of our power over nature—particularly in medical science—has realized healing and public health in measures totally unattainable in pre-scientific ages. And even where science is a very knowledge-is-power type of enterprise, and carefully concerned with objective facts, it is also inescapably a *human* enterprise. Michael Polanyi's *Personal Knowledge* beautifully notices the manner in which scientific discovery is always an integrative process where the internal pole of socially situated human meaning and the external pole of observed nature are in continual dialogue with each other.[4]

4. Polanyi, *Personal Knowledge*. See also Polanyi's beautiful little text *The*

Fourthly, *a pervasive background feature of our worldview is the incoherent collage of all four of the West's deep historically embedded theories of magic.* Of course, the dominant social theories of magic assumed by our actual way of life are the supernatural theory (for people with sensibilities more or less aligned with modern Western religion) and the anti-magic theory (for post-religious agnostics and atheists). Yet, via suitably Westernized forms of Eastern philosophy, some resurgence of animist magic, integrated, often enough, with scientistic atheism, is rather fashionable. But when it comes to Platonist magic, this lives primarily in the realm of fantasy. Here the giants of twentieth-century fantasy—Lewis and Tolkien—were conscious advocates of the imaginative recovery of the Platonist sensibility. While Rowling is probably less consciously aware of her metaphysical commitments than the two fantasy-writing Oxford Dons were, she is still deeply intuitively Platonist in the stories she tells, though she certainly leans into animism and supernaturalism as well. So sociologically, all four theories of magic profoundly shape different aspects of our life-world, and in this sense we obviously live in a high—if remarkably complex—age of magic.

Getting to the bottom of how magic works in our life-world, and what its strengths and limitations are, is a demanding challenge. When it comes to thinking about magic itself, we will need to be aware of the life-world filters that modernity places on us. We will need to understand how we came to think of reality as largely confined to only those things science can see if we are going to think clearly about whether magic itself is real or not. To do all this, we cannot avoid taking a pretty serious plunge into the strange waters of the intellectual history of magic and Western science. There is some hard thinking to do in a book on magic and reality in an age of science. But I shall try to make the difficult parts as concrete and as jargon-free (or at least jargon-explained) as I can.

So let us now ask, what is magic?

Tacit Dimension for further thoughts on the manner in which the actual practice of science itself pushes back against reductive scientism.

LESSON TWO

FOUR THEORIES OF MAGIC

Magic is concerned with the shimmering cosmic meanings and the dangerous and life-giving powers that lie just below the surface of the apparent. There are four basic theories about magic.[1]

The first two theories are ancient. According to one theory, magic is entirely located *within* nature, and Nature itself is divine. Here there is nothing about nature that is not alive with its own energies, powers, and intentions, for everything natural is magical. To this theory, we too are both natural and magical. Our own selves, words, and artefacts are also alive with magical intentions and powers. We can call this the **animist theory of magic** because "animated" means "alive."

According to the other ancient theory, magic—though saturating nature—has its origin from *beyond* nature. To this theory, the world that we can touch and see is *derived from* and *dependent*

---

1. I am heavily indebted to some yet-to-be-published work by John Milbank on science and magic for the four theories of magic I will use in this book. Even so, Professor Milbank's understanding of the four main ways of thinking about the metaphysics of nature in Western intellectual history is more nuanced and technical than how I describe them. So whilst one should not judge Professor Milbank's work by my work, nevertheless—and with his gracious permission—I want to acknowledge my debt to him here.

on a higher, immaterial reality. Without this higher reality the ever-changing observable world in which we live would be a field of incomprehensible flux and contingency. We can see meaning, order, and value in nature because nature itself is dependent on the intrinsic meaning, the eternal order, and the primal goodness of divine reason. To this second theory, there is a transcendent and intellective "beyond" that orders and sustains the natural world into which we are born. We can call this the **Platonist theory of magic**, after the most famous Ancient Greek philosopher who held this stance, Plato.

About five-hundred years ago a new theory of magic was born. The origins of this third theory lie in complex discussions within medieval metaphysics and theology. One aspect of that backstory is a strong interest in modifying the Platonist understanding of nature. By the fourteenth century most of the leading thinkers of that age took it for granted that early medieval Christian Platonism did not adequately appreciate the self-standing and concrete "whatness" (*quiddity*) of ordinary things in the world. Order, meaning, essence, and value *within* tangible nature was now being thought of as fundamental *to* nature. In contrast, the high Platonist outlooks of early medieval realism saw reason, meaning, and goodness as gifted to nature, from *beyond* nature, in a way that made spatiotemporal nature inherently dependent on eternal divinity.

From the fourteenth to the sixteenth century, powerful thinkers sought ways of understanding the time-and-space-located world of particular material things as a *self-standing* reality. To do this, Western theologians eventually developed the theory of a sharply separated cosmos. In this strictly two-tiered arrangement, there is a self-standing, purely natural world (*natura pura*) in one order of reality, and there is a fully discrete supernatural order of reality, outside of nature.

The sixteenth-century idea of *natura pura*—where a self-standing nature needs no ongoing divine grace to be what it is—was an astonishing development in the theory of magic.[2] In

---

2. See Dupré, *Passage to Modernity* for a fascinating history of the rise of

this way of thinking, "pure nature" did *not* require participation in divine Being or transcendent forms from beyond nature. As this outlook developed, God came to be thought of as an *external, super-natural* Agent, who was the maker of nature, but who had no ongoing role to play within nature (apart from the occasional miracle).

If one compares this new outlook with the older Platonist Christian outlook, you can see that this third theory of magic entails a radically new conception of both Deity and of creation.[3] The new theory is a very strongly *dualist* outlook where an earthly nature is decisively separated out from a heavenly supernature. Further, natural things no longer have any magical mystery about them—they have become concretely knowable objects in the material space-time world. From here it became possible for the good Christian thinkers of late medieval and early modern times to entirely de-mystify and de-magic nature. In this way innovations in Christian theology gave rise to modern science. We can call this dramatic innovation the **supernatural theory of magic**.

As the modern scientific age developed, a new theory about the nature of nature gradually arose out of the supernatural theory. If nature does not need supernature to be what it is, and if nature can be understood in a purely natural way, then the supernatural becomes *functionally superfluous* to our knowledge of the world. It is now possible to discard the supernatural (and the magical, and the metaphysical) as outside of a true knowledge of tangible reality. It is now possible to think that religion, magic, and transcendence-concerned philosophy are mere fictions. This trajectory leads to a fourth outlook: the **anti-magical theory of magic**.

I am aware that this self-eating label is a bit awkward, but no other label will fit if we are interested in magic. That is, the rejection of the reality of magic itself is, actually, a potent negative

---

the kind of thought categories—including *natura pura*—that were necessary for modern science to emerge.

3. See Oliver, *Creation: A Guide for the Perplexed* for very helpful exposition of how different modern conceptions of God and creation are, when compared to patristic and medieval outlooks within Western Christianity.

theory of magic. To say "magic does not exist" implies a certain view of reality and a certain conception of magic as not only outside of nature (as it is for the supernatural theory of magic) but as not real, and not possible, in any sense. Magic becomes pure fantasy. *Natura pura* nature is no longer the lower level of a two-tiered cosmos, but non-magical matter is now *all that there is*. By the eighteenth century it is quite possible for renegade free thinkers to think of reality itself as fully defined by a reductively mechanical and materialist naturalism.

The above very quick spin through the four big theories of magic gives you just the barest conceptual scaffolding. We will give the animist and Platonist theories of magic more attention as we go. But at the start of this investigation, we should give a little more attention to understanding the two modern theories of magic.

It is important to grasp how theologically defined the third theory is, and how dominant this outlook was in the early modern period. It is equally important to grasp that the fourth theory develops naturally from the third theory, though it did not really gain much influence until the nineteenth century. These two views largely shape the way we think about magic now, even though—actually—the two premodern theories of magic are still alive and well in the deep back-furnishings of our minds.

SUPERNATURAL THEOLOGY AND ANTI-MAGIC SCIENTISM: MOTHER AND CHILD

By the eighteenth century—thanks to the rise of *natura pura*, the ditching of Aristotle's metaphysics, and the amazing success of Newtonian physics—it was possible to think of the physical universe as one huge and entirely natural machine, like a clock. It was increasingly assumed by the learned that this machine could be understood and mastered by experimental and mathematical knowledge. The old ways of approaching the darkly glowing mysteries, the Creator-embedded wonders, and the quasi-divine animate powers of nature could now be set aside. As the Enlightenment matured, premodern ideas of a divinely given moral order embedded within nature could now be thought of as outdated. New, more scientific ways of thinking about right and wrong were invented. Modern theorists set about calculating the hedonistic utility of various choices, carefully weighing quantified pleasures and pains against each other in order to re-think the value and meaning of things within a purely natural reality. What we now call science began to pull away from older conceptions of philosophy, ethics, and theology as knowledge became purely natural and practical. This development did not make an anti-magical rejection of the supernatural necessary, but it certainly made it possible.

It is important to remember that it was theological innovations that produced the supernatural theory of magic, which in turn made the rise of the scientific age and the anti-magical outlook possible. It is worth briefly dwelling on this because the deep historical relationships between theology, magic, science, and modernity are often not well understood.

Historically, Western religion causes the decline of pre-modern magical thinking about nature and promotes the rise of modern science. Academics who study these things understand this well. But if you have a less specialized education, this may seem counter-intuitive. For what is called "the conflict thesis"—the idea that science and religion are, by definition, in a state of perpetual conflict—has powerful cultural clout, despite it being historically indefensible.[4]

The theological invention of the idea of "pure nature," as separated out from the supernatural realm, is the womb of modern science. Once modern science was born, it had, for some centuries, a warm and filial relationship with its theological mother. At least three seventeenth-century theological bearings, within the sixteenth-century housing of the supernatural theory of magic, enabled the productive wheels of early modern science to spin. Firstly, thinking of nature as entirely discrete from divinity, we readily came to believe that nature could be fully understood by entirely natural means. Mundane observation (experiment) and

4. See, for example, Numbers, *Galileo Goes to Jail, and Other Myths about Science and Religion*.

commonsense logic (mathematics) were now all one needed to understand everything there was to know about nature. Secondly, holding that Man was divinely commissioned to rule the earth (Gen 1:28), the scientific mastery of nature and the technological bending of her powers to our own use was seen as a clear religious responsibility. Historically, scientific pragmatism has a theological justification. Thirdly, early modern thinkers largely assumed that even if nature was a purely material and mechanical machine, we ourselves stood out from nature. For uniquely within the natural world, we had reasoning and supernatural souls. (Just this one bit of supernature gets smuggled into *natura pura* nature.) The detached objectivity of the scientific gaze treats nature as in some manner discrete from our own knowing minds, for theological reasons.

Distinctive forms of Christian theology and early modern science were comfortably co-dependent in the early modern period. But over time, the modern naturalist trajectory that was latent within the supernatural theory really did come into conflict with the theological grounds that birthed it. The idea that nature has no essential intellective meanings, no qualitative truths, no immaterial animate powers, no sacred secrets, and no magic is part and parcel of the dualist cosmology of the supernaturalist outlook. But the idea that this sort of purely natural nature is all that there is—the distinctly modern and metaphysically materialist form of naturalism—dispenses with the supernatural upper level of the two-tiered cosmos entirely.

By the 1840s, powerful intellectual streams within modern naturalism had evolved into a reductively materialist outlook on reality. Once you arrive at this juncture, then you really are cooking up a serious conflict between post-Enlightenment materialist scientism and early modern supernatural religion. At this point we can see that even though the conflict thesis is historically wrong as a blanket statement about science and religion, it is not entirely wrong. Indeed, it is no surprise that by the early twentieth century the conflict thesis became a motherhood truth to people whose outlook on the world was now formed by nineteenth-century Progressive materialist thinking.

Under the banner of modern naturalism our fourth theory about the nature of reality comes onto the scene. If only the purely natural is deemed to be scientifically real, and if only what science can tell us about nature is valid *knowledge*, then—as far as practical scientific realism is concerned—both the supernatural and the magical become redundant. It is no surprise, then, that a culturally maturing science could decide it was time to leave home, renounce its theological mother, and kill its divine father. From the eighteenth century on we start to see knowledge separate out from belief, and religion starts to drift away from knowable practical reality, along with magic. We start to see magic not only as separated out from nature, but also as dismissed with the supernatural from here-and-now reality itself. After such a dismissal, any serious belief in magic, or anything supernatural, can now be reasonably thought of as a childish delusion that has no place in the scientific age. Uneducated magical folk beliefs and scientifically impossible religious doctrines were now thought of as belonging to the same genus. Magic and religion could now both be tossed into the bin of superstition.[5]

Interestingly, while there certainly was a good deal of cultural euphoria about casting off the chains of superstition during the Enlightenment, losing the theological bearings of early modern science had a range of profound and unexpected cultural impacts. After some of our pioneering thinkers had decisively shifted away from any sort of supernatural understanding of reality, we ourselves became naturalized within a purely material reality. In this emerging cultural vision of ourselves, we no longer have eternal souls, we are no longer created in the image of God, we no longer stand out from nature. As Nietzsche points out, the cultural killing of God is like wiping away the horizon *of our own meaning* with a sponge. Who are we in this brave new purely material world?

---

5. Transcendence concerned philosophy also finds itself readily thrown into the bin of unprovable speculation. Even so, rationalists and idealists make a number of valiant attempts at asserting themselves in the modern period.

The modern anti-magic theory arises out of the naturalistic fulfillment and the supernatural redundance of the modern nature/supernature dualist theory of magic. The supernatural theory of magic is the mother of the anti-magical theory of magic. But once we arrive at an anti-magical outlook, anything that does not have a material and scientifically verifiable explanation does not exist. Hence, anything that appears to be of a non-material nature—such as the intrinsic dignity of a human life, or consciousness—is not really unexplainable by cold hard science. This means that human dignity and consciousness may *appear* to us to be non-material "magical" realities, but actually, we know they are necessarily—in the final analysis—either cultural fantasies that have been developed for biological reasons or entirely physical processes. This is a theory that interprets anything "magical" in an unmasking and deflationary way. This is not just a stance that has no interest in magic, it is a stance that refuses to treat any aspect of reality in a magical way and that actively interprets our experience of reality in anti-magical terms.

Bearing in mind the intimate historical relationship between the supernatural and the anti-magical theories of magic, let us now re-cap on the central features of the four theories of magic outlined so far. The differences in the way these outlooks understand the relationship between immanence and transcendence is particularly important to grasp.

IMMANENCE AND TRANSCENDENCE, EXPLAINED WITH A ROSE

Here are our four theories of magic:

1. Animist magic is a magic of pure immanence. Here the wonder and mystery of the world is firmly situated *within* and comes *from* Nature.

2. Platonist magic is also a magic manifest in natural immanence, yet the wonder and mystery of the world transcends

nature. Here magic is still decisively expressed *within* nature, yet magic itself comes from *beyond* nature.

3. Supernatural magic is carefully isolated from the non-magical immanence of nature. Here magic is set apart from nature and firmly placed within the sphere of the supernatural. Effectively, magic is *cast out* of nature.

4. To anti-magical materialism, magic and the supernatural *do not exist*. Here any appeal to magic, or to anything "beyond" the reductively materialist gaze of what science can see, is delusional.

To clarify, "immanence" means *embedded within nature*, and "transcendence" refers to *a higher order of reality* that is both *prior to* and *beyond* material nature. It is important to understand what these two words mean so that we can understand the differences between the four theories of magic we are considering. To grasp this, consider a rose.

To the magically fascinated observer of a rose, the magic of its beauty will be thought of as originating entirely *within* the living plant to the **immanent-minded** animist theorist. It is a living and magical beauty, but entirely natural. To the animist theory, nothing transcends nature—*nature is all there is, though it is magical.* Spirits and gods—or even "a God"—might be part of an animist perspective, but these spirits and spiritual powers do not transcend nature.

To the **Platonist**-minded theorist, the beauty of the rose will also be **immanent** to the particular plant, but beauty itself will **transcend** that particular flower, and the flower will be understood as participating in some divine and eternal quality of Beauty that has its origin and ongoing reality *beyond* the transient flower. Magic within nature is something that is situated *between* imminence and transcendence, and is intimately entangled in both immanence and transcendence. Here, we cannot know any pure transcendence or any pure immanence, but material nature is not ultimate; it is dependent on some immaterial higher reality that transcends the natural world.

To the **supernatural** theorist, the rose is an entirely natural, **immanent**, and non-magical thing in the world: it has no intrinsic meaning or value in itself. And yet, the human mind observing the rose through brain-processed bodily sensations is **supernatural**; meaning and value—as functions of soul or spirit—are thus also supernatural. So the human mind indirectly communes with the supernatural divine Mind, by means of the beauty of the rose. For beauty and value *in minds* (where minds are *not* an objective feature of nature) is supernaturally apparent to the sensitive mind in observing natural phenomena. Yet magic itself is decisively separated from an entirely imminent nature here.

To the modern de-magical vision—**anti-magical** materialism—"beauty" is simply a subjective human gloss that does not exist in or beyond the rose at all. Reality itself is here understood as **entirely immanent** and purely material, such that all meanings and qualities only *really* exist as subjective by-products of matter, within our brains. This is an entirely immanent view of reality.

	Animist	Platonist	Supernatural	Anti-magical
Magic is immanent in nature	X	X	–	–
Magic transcends nature	–	X	X	–

"PURE NATURE" AND MODERN DISENCHANTMENT

Hopefully you now have a clearer idea of how each of these four different outlooks on nature are deeply defined by their particular understanding of the relationship between immanence and transcendence. It should also be clear that our two modern theories share a radically immanent conception of nature.

Modern knowledge is embedded in a "pure nature" vision of reality. The *pure* bit here means that transcendence and the supernatural are entirely purged from how we now understand a valid (i.e., scientific) knowledge of natural reality. In other words, the distinctly modern view of nature is exclusively immanent, material, temporal, and metaphysically self-standing.

Modern science arises out of a "pure nature" conception of nature. In many ways, the flourishing of modern science and technology is a wonderful development that we are very pleased about; we know how material things work, what there actually is to know, and how to govern a wide range of natural processes, far in advance of any previous system of natural knowledge and technological power. And yet, qualities and meanings, and religious and transcendent longings, have not disappeared. But we now cannot think of these non-scientifically definable categories as compatible with a true knowledge of nature, or even—in their own terms— as real. In many ways, this troubles us. It looks like our scientific knowledge and our marvelous technology has disenchanted the world. The meaning and value of nature and of our own humanity is now strangely difficult for us to treat as real. But this is a very complex area. We must now consider in what respects modern disenchantment really did happen, and in what respects, it did not happen.

LESSON THREE

DISENCHANTMENT HAPPENED

M ax Weber was one of the great founding thinkers of the
modern discipline of sociology. He had fascinating and interesting things to say about religion, magic, science, and meaning
in the context of modern society. In 1918, Weber announced that
because of a long process of rationalization and intellectualization,
twentieth-century Western society unavoidably saw the whole
world as disenchanted.[1] Weber's German word that we translate
into English as "disenchantment" is *Entzauberung*; literally, "de-
magicing." Weber's thinking around disenchantment is richly complex, even contradictory, but what I take to be the most important
aspect of his meaning is that we no longer *experience* the world
as alive with spirits and living elemental forces. As will become
apparent, I think aspects of Weber's understanding of disenchantment are seriously problematic, but in very broad terms, his understanding of our experience of the world is obviously correct. As
a modern Western person, I do not *experience* spirit beings in the
river, I do not have the *experience* of ongoing fellowship with my
ancestors and the animate powers of the animals and land. Now I
might believe in spirits, or not, and I might have religious beliefs

1. See Weber's famous essay "Science as a Vocation," in Gerth and Mills,
(eds.), *From Max Weber: Essays in Sociology*, 129–56.

19

about God and the supernatural, or not, but Weber is interested in *experience* when he talks of disenchantment.

For example, I know First Nation Australians who do not—in the modern sense—*believe* unprovable animist doctrines. They do not believe in spirit companions or the presence of their ancestors; no—they simply *experience* them. For the way we understand and experience the world is embedded in the shared meanings and practices of our culture and language. But if our language, stories, and way of life separates out "the supernatural" from "the natural," then what can be experienced as real is only the "purely" natural. Here—whether spirits and animate forces are actually there or not—we do not experience spirits. If we have a linear cultural conception of time, then, to us, the present (whatever that is) is radically isolated from the past and the future in our *experience* of the world. If we have an atomic individualist conception of the self and organize our social world around providing freedoms for that self, then to us the relational web of our lives and identities are essentially backgrounded to our awareness of ourselves. There is nothing sharply true or false about this, but the fact is, if you grow up speaking German, that language automatically makes sense to you, but other languages do not. Language here is not just a set of coded symbols transmitting information; it is a set of meanings. The meanings of the self, of nature, of spirit, of time, for example, are given to us in the deep cultural formation of our language.

If, for whatever reason, you don't experience the world within the acceptable reality parameters of the cultural context to which you belong, you need to have a pretty good excuse, or else you will be deemed mad. Original Australians have a largely acceptable excuse to not see reality in entirely the same way that the colonizing European culture imposes, but anyone else who hears voices at the waterhole will have a psychosis and need treatment. Now, of course, some people really do have a psychosis, and I mean no disrespect to the modern science of psychology, but Weber's point is sociological, not psychological.

One of the *Pirates of the Caribbean* movies puts forward Weber's sociological insight in a beautifully dramatic manner. The film seems to be set in the eighteenth century. In one scene, the legendary Kraken lies dead on the beach. It represents a world passing away, a world of curses, monsters, gods, and magically layered realms of space and time full of strange cracks between the living and the dead. This old world was being pushed out of our experience of reality by the East India Company and the British Empire, as it surged forward in charting all areas of the map and bringing all the treasures of nature into the storehouse of colonial conquest. The movie is imaginatively set in the twilight zone between two orders of cultural reality. There is some crossover, but in the end the monsters give way to science, magic gives way to administrative and military power, the spiritually high realms of enchanted love and the demonic low realms of curses and untamable chaotic natural powers both give way to middle-class romance and a strong legal system.

Something that really happened in the development of "the self" within modern Western culture is what Charles Taylor calls "buffering."[2] That is, the self of late modernity becomes strangely insulated from both nature and transcendence. The self finds itself locked up in its own echo chamber of meaning. This, I think, is one of the things that Weber was trying to identify in his notion of disenchantment. Strangely, our lived reality has become isolated, not within pure nature, but within the "iron cage" of the purely human and culturally constructed world. Part of this has to do with the fact that the dominant modern conception of knowledge is a decisively instrumental "maker's knowledge." The knowledge we construct in the scientific age through our experiments, our theories, and most of all, through our technologies, has become our large open window onto reality. On the other hand, the older windows of more directly responsive adaptation to the givenness of nature, and to the transcendent mysteries that shape the world beyond the scope of our own interests and powers, have largely shut. We try to re-find nature through various forms of tourism into nature, and we try to re-find transcendence through imagination. Science itself is still some sort of window onto nature. But

2. See Taylor, *A Secular Age*.

our windows onto transcendence are now very hard to open. We try and find big-M Meaning through religion (for some), non-religious spiritual experience (for others), and through the strangely liturgical rituals of secular consumerism (for all of us). We find that an anti-magical metaphysic of pure immanence is settling down, like a heavy fog, over the old landscape of the West's fading supernatural religious consciousness. The transcendent stars that used to guide us are now invisible. The semi-animist creatures of mystical natural powers are no longer concrete in the imagination's eyes, but have become shadows in the fog, mere figments of our own making. In the half-light of this new metaphysical climate, the flat unmeaning of all reality beyond our own making and the purely constructed meanings of our personal and cultural making becomes increasingly culturally oppressive. Driven by a sort of sordid desperation, our "troubled youth" resort to escapist narcotic states and the attempt to find some sort of self-transcending experiential mythos in our bodily appetites and heightened awareness states—sex, speed, danger. . . . But because of the way our post-religious purely immanent cosmos forms us to experience reality, we cannot acknowledge any meaning that is not simply made up within the world of our own knowledge and power constructions. We live within an age consciously defined by human *poiesis* and constructed *mythos*, as never before.

Let us zoom out a bit.

The invention of *natura pura* has given us license to stand over nature with an instrumental and controlling intent to an extent unprecedented in the history of humanity. This move has—ironically—also buffered human meaning, making it strangely discrete from both nature and transcendence, and making meaning itself a purely cultural construct. This development would not have been possible without the supernatural/natural delineation of our modern two-tiered theory of the cosmos. Yet once we come to see and shape the world in this modern way, the normal *experiences* native to the older outlook becomes increasingly incomprehensible. The old magical frameworks of common experience regarding transcendence and nature no longer have a living and practical place in our social reality.

I will now try and do something that is really rather risky. I will try and quickly unpack the relationship between shared outlooks of experience and deep cultural frameworks of meaning using a philosopher and a theologian.

The most brilliant philosophical thinker of the eighteenth-century Scottish Enlightenment was David Hume. If you read his critiques of miracles and natural religion, you are likely to find them very persuasive. There are a two reasons this. Firstly, Hume was a powerful original thinker and a master of literary expression and persuasive reasoning. Secondly, he just makes sense to us, for we now think in much the same way that he pioneered.

Hume is a very modern thinker who maintains a skeptical and empirical stance as regards believable knowledge. Hume trusts no truth foundations embedded in either unprovable metaphysical speculation or faith-premised religious first principals. Hume also reasons from a modern naturalistic conception of how we know our world. Thinking in this way, Hume powerfully argues that only mathematical relations of ideas and probable facts of common (purely natural) experience are admissible as valid. Once we have accepted this much, it is almost inevitable that we will agree with Hume and find any sort of reasonable defense of natural theology and miracles to be impossible.

I want to zone in on how Hume experiences the world and contrast that with how a medieval theologian—Saint Thomas Aquinas—experienced the world.

Part of what Hume does is critique what looks like some natural theology proofs for the existence of God by Aquinas. Now I don't want to get involved in either Humean skepticism or Thomistic theology here, but what I want to draw attention to is that Hume and Aquinas experience reality in very different ways, and this experiential difference is a decisive difference between them. Aquinas reasons in a manner consistent with the way he experiences reality as understood within a medieval Christian Neo-Platonist set of metaphysical assumptions about the relationship between God—as the ground of being—and creation. Hume reasons in a manner consistent with the way he experiences reality as understood by modern skeptical empiricism.

Hume brilliantly shows us what sort of trouble you get into when you try and establish that it is reasonable to believe in "a God"[3] by modern naturalistic means. But precisely this modern attempt to *experience* God rationalistically and empirically, and this eighteenth-century deistic conception of what *a* God is (which Hume has in his crosshairs), is foreign to Thomas' medieval Christian theology and worship.[4] For the *experience* of the Person of God, as grasped within patristic and medieval modes of Christian understanding, has no connection to what Hume does *not* experience. To Aquinas, God was the *ground of* being, not *a* being *in* the world, not *a* being *in* heaven, and not deism's abstractly rational and empirically demonstrable Supreme Being.[5]

Let us not get tangled in medieval theology and modern atheism here. All I want to point out is that even though a significant prong of Hume's critique of natural theology *looks like* it is a critique of Aquinas' five ways, the "God" Hume is critiquing is not recognizable to the experience of God that Aquinas took

3. Hume, *Dialogue concerning Natural Religion*, 38. Here Hume is making an ironic polemic affirmation that the truth of "the being of a God" is certain. Hume will argue that even if we take "a God" as certain, no feature of the nature of that being can be demonstrated with a natural theology grounded in a modern skeptical empiricism.

4. See Hart, *The Experience of God*. Indeed, old fashioned orthodox Christian belief rather agrees with most of what modern atheism denies about "God." This is because classically modern, deistic and naturalistic conceptions of "God" are entirely unrecognizable to orthodox Christian belief and experience. See also Banks, *And Man Created God*.

5. For those of you who are familiar with Christian theology, the *mystery* of the incarnation is precisely that the second person of the Trinity becomes, for a short time, a being in the world. This is a mystery. That is, God is not understood as "a god" in any of the three great Abrahamic theological traditions. So in Christian theology, the impossibility of understanding God as "a being" is held in hard paradoxical tension with the deity of the concrete, historical, enfleshed man, Jesus of Nazareth. Several very productive lines of heretical Christian theology are largely defined by attempting to resolve or obliterate this paradox.

for granted. For Aquinas was a thirteenth-century Christian who did not experience the world, or knowledge, or God, in the same manner that eighteenth-century deism did, let alone Hume's eighteenth-century skeptical empiricism. Thomas Aquinas *experienced* a world where the divine grounds of being saturated creation and gave a transcendent horizon to all immanent experience. Aquinas never experienced a two-tiered cosmos or *natura pura* modern knowledge, and so his reasoning makes no sense to people who cannot even imagine the way he experienced the world.

I mean no disrespect to the astonishing intellect of David Hume by making the above observation, but he and Saint Thomas Aquinas inhabit different languages of meaning and experience reality in different ways, and so they do not deeply communicate with each other. Now they can't both be right. Fundamentally, reality is either embedded in the divine or it is not, but that Thomas' reasoning does not make sense to Hume is a function of Thomas' experience of the world being incompatible with Hume's experience of the world, it is not a mere silly fault in Thomas' reasoning, or a merely superficial misreading of medieval thinking on Hume's part. This is a first-order disagreement about experience.

Once we embrace the modern metaphysical vision of a purely natural nature (as consistent with seventeenth-century supernatural thinking), Hume's outlook corresponds neatly to the way we experience the world. But Hume is right; if I adhere to a supernatural theory of magic, then the separation of the natural from the supernatural does indeed make the supernatural functionally redundant to my ordinary experience of reality. The only difference between the supernaturalist and the anti-magical naturalist is in the non-provable interpretation of the *meaning* of scientifically knowable nature and scientifically unknowable supernature; the *experience* of un-magical nature and valid scientific reasoning is shared by both outlooks.

At this point we should stop and consider how powerful and persuasive the reality vision of *natura pura* is, and how believable both modern theories of magic are that fall out of it. For it is this power and believability that gives disenchantment its deep cultural influence over Western modernity, particularly in the academy.

Very briefly put, the idea of *natura pura* nature arises out of innovations produced by highly creative and intelligent thinkers as they struggled to resolve difficulties inherent in medieval realism, in medieval conceptions of being, and in the medieval doctrine of prime matter. These innovations were all pursued from within the deep and abiding interest in metaphysics, language, and logic that characterized medieval philosophy and theology. Which is to say that the modern concept of nature (and hence, modern science) has deep medieval roots. This accounts for why we find the medieval era so imaginatively fascinating and also have such a prejudicial loathing of it. For scientific modernity has disowned its medieval parents, and has constructed its origin myth as a triumphant rebellion against its doddering and oppressive elders. Of course, it was not only intellectual innovations that produced modernity, it was also innovations of political, religious, and technological power—but those innovations are integral with the intellectual developments that produced the modern scientific age.

I will not try to give you seven brief lessons explaining the medieval origins of modernity here.[6] Let us skip ahead to the seventeenth century, when all the innovations out of which the scientific revolution arises are firmly in place.

The first point to note is that nearly all the major seventeenth-century fathers of the scientific revolution were Christians of one sort or another. This means they adhered to some form of the two-tiered cosmology where nature is firmly separated from supernature, and yet the supernatural is still held to be more primary to reality than the natural. This is the original worldview of modern science. Scientists and mathematicians today who are Christians and who seek to align modern Christian theology with modern science—thinkers such as the two Oxford Professors Alister McGrath and John Lennox, for instance—are right to maintain that

6. The medieval roots of modernity are beautifully traced in two very helpful books by Robert Pasnau: *Metaphysical Themes 1274–1671* and *After Certainty: A History of Our Epistemic Ideals and Illusions.*

their outlook is both thoroughly consistent with modern science, and thoroughly in keeping with doctrinally orthodox renditions of modern Christian theology. Here God gives nature its own being and sets the laws of nature in place, and then—in a manner of speaking—takes His leave of nature and goes to (supernatural) heaven. To this outlook, it is quite possible for God to supernaturally intervene in nature should God so chose, and to extra-naturally commune with the believer's soul at will. Here, the mathematical and contingent coherence of the natural order is given to nature from beyond nature, but for all practical and realistic purposes, we understand the creative work of God through the modern scientific method. Here nature itself is explicitly not holy or sacred such that the taboo-free technological appropriation of nature so characteristic of modernity is fully at home to this supernaturalist outlook. And we would not have modern science if it were not for Christians such as Galileo, Descartes, and Bacon, and Unitarians like Newton, who decoded the letters of the divine Mathematician inscribed in the most universal and foundational writings of the "book of nature."

Yet anyone who studies Isaac Newton closely will quickly come to realize the Keynes was correct to describe that seventeenth-century Arian fellow of Trinity College not as the first great scientist, but as the last great magician. Newton wrote considerably more on biblical numerology, non-Trinitarian church history, alchemy, and biblical criticism than he did on physics and mathematics. To Newton, science, theology, and alchemy were a unity, even if his science employed a decisively modern mathematical, rationalist, and experimental methodology. Newton's understanding of the relations between a *natura pura* immanent nature, and the supernatural—as with most pre-nineteenth-century natural philosophers—is highly complex, and it does *not* fit the categories of modern materialistic naturalism. For here the supernatural ground of nature *was* cosmologically primary—even if it could be functionally discrete from rational and empirical science—in a manner that is very different to how nineteenth-century anti-magical materialism makes the immanent world its own (and the only knowable) cosmological reality.

A supernaturalist theory of magic remains compatible with the scientific age and an instrumental attitude towards nature, and it would be facile to think that this is not a very serious position. Indeed, this stance enjoys some very hard-hitting contemporary philosophical advocates, such as Alvin Plantinga. And yet clearly, the Humean move to render the supernatural functionally super-fluous to empirical observation and rational calculation is also deeply compatible with a *natura pura* metaphysics. Because modern science arises out of a Christian European knowledge culture (Western universities were set up by the Catholic Church in the Middle Ages) and because most of the pioneers of the new learning were Christians, it took some centuries before an anti-religious rejection of any sort of supernatural realism could produce a re-ductively materialist and anti-magical stance. This fourth outlook only really matured in the nineteenth century. In the 1870s two en-terprising Americans—John Draper and Andrew White—can be credited with inventing the notion of a perpetual and ancient war between science and religion. As already mentioned, this conflict thesis has very little respect among historians of modern science, but it has stuck in the popular imagination.[7]

It is clear that the intellectual credibility and scientific use-fulness of both the supernaturalist and anti-magical stances give deep cultural credibility to the disenchantment that Weber de-scribes. The clarity and power of our modern scientific knowledge presupposes a *natura pura* perspective on nature and reality, so unsurprisingly, the *natura pura* perspective is also culturally clear and powerful to us. Disenchantment is deeply tied up with this perspective. But is the matter all sewn up? Can animist and Pla-tonist understandings of magic and nature no longer be treated as live options? Or are there regions of the modern mind—perhaps to one side of our knowledge-and-power culture—where *natura pura* has not really had much impact?

---

7. See Harrison, *The Territories of Science and Religion*.

DISENCHANTMENT DID NOT HAPPEN

Disenchantment is a myth. Myths are very culturally powerful things, and one would misunderstand what a myth is entirely if one thought that we of the modern age do not have our own and distinctly modern myths. Of those myths, disenchantment is one of the big ones.

The Myth of Disenchantment is a fascinating recent book by Jason Josephson-Storm. In this book, Professor Josephson-Storm points out that Weber's part in constructing the myth of disenchantment is tangled in some really delicious ironies. For one thing, Weber was talking about the de-magicing of the world at the same time that there was an occult craze raging in many of the elite intellectual circles in which he turned. Some of the most famous European scientists of the early twentieth century—Marie Curie, Jean Baptiste Perrin, Charles Richet—were deeply fascinated by paranormal phenomena. This was going on all over Europe and the English-speaking world: think of the studied interest in séances, mysticism, mind-energy, Eastern religion, etc., of thinkers such as Sigmund Freud, William James, Henri Bergson, and Erwin Schrödinger. It is a complex point of Weberian studies to try and piece together how Weber integrates (or does not integrate) his familiarity with this widespread and very serious scientific fascination with the paranormal, and his theory of disenchantment. He is too sophisticated a sociologist not to understand the relationships between modern science and modern myth, and he was certainly aware of the ongoing interest in magic in his own circle of close intellectual friends. We will not try to resolve that delicate scholarly matter here. But let me quickly unpack to you the manner in which disenchantment did not happen.

As pointed out in the third lesson, disenchantment is deeply consistent with the assumed *natura pura* metaphysics of modernity, and is compatible with both a supernaturalist and an antimagical theory of magic. So in this sense, the myth stands firm within the social reality of modernity. However, features of our normal experience that are now anomalous with the distinctive realism of both modern theories of magic have not gone away. This produces a fascinating background dissonance between our knowledge and our belief, our science and our imagination, our theory and our experience. The way we of the modern world understand what "natural" objective facts are sets up an unavoidable dissonance between reality and its meaning and value.

John Locke was one of the great seventeenth-century fathers of British empiricism. To Locke, only what he took to be the primary qualities of physical things—extension, figure, motion, solidity, number—could be said to have a definite reality that was independent of the mind of the human observer. Primary and objective reality is thus real, whatever we think of it, and this makes it more real than our subjective and secondary impressions and interpretations of perceived reality. This separation between a primary factual world of bare objects and all the subjectively perceived secondary qualities of things, renders objective reality itself as brute fact, without meaning. Here values, purposes, meaning, and metaphysical orders are—for all scientific and practical purposes—not real features of objective reality. And yet, in our actual human experience, value, meaning, and purpose are fundamental to our ordinary lives. But are these "secondary" qualities not really real, and is their sense of importance merely a matter of personal or cultural interpretation that has no solid grounding in the way reality really is? Our conception of meaningless objective facts sets up a serious cultural dissonance problem between our scientific knowledge of reality and our subjective experience of meaning and value.

This then is how the case for disenchantment needs to be nuanced. As a *mythos* at one with the assumed supernaturalist and anti-magical metaphysics of scientific modernity, disenchantment is a powerful life-world defining myth, ordering our understanding and experience of reality. However, this is in important regards *a false mythology*. For actually, enchantment has not vanished from our ordinary experience of reality. What has really happened is that our understanding of *where* enchantment *is* has moved— under the conditions of scientific modernity—entirely out of the categories of knowledge and factual reality, and completely into the categories of imagination and subjectivity.

This raises some very interesting questions. What, then, is the metaphysical status of human imagination and subjectivity? What is the reality (or not) of the magic that we find in imagination and subjectivity?

SUBJECTIVITY AND ENCHANTMENT

Søren Kierkegaard was a Danish philosopher of the nineteenth century. Kierkegaard pointed out that an objective understanding of material facts has never been a pathway to any ultimate truth.[1] This is common knowledge to anyone who has seriously tried to get a fixed and final truth out of science.[2] Science provides us with useful, approximate, and revisable knowledge. A good physical theory about how things really are—as checked, confirmed, and revised by experimental observation—is always a theory that opens up further questions and experiments, and attempting to answer these further questions often changes (and sometimes replaces)

1. Kierkegaard, *Concluding Postscript to the Philosophical Fragments*, 9–49.
2. See Chalmers, *What Is This Thing Called Science?*

the initial theory over time. In short, one is always proceeding (hopefully) towards truth, but never finally arriving at truth, via scientific knowledge. Modern science is also explicitly limited in its scope to the measurable and mathematically modelable aspects of physical reality.

Our objective knowledge of the physical world—science—obviously has a good working relationship with how physical things really are. And science is wonderful for those things that it is good at. But to try and use modern science to find ultimate truth, even about physical reality, let alone the true meaning of things, is to misunderstand the nature of science and to misuse it. The light of our experimental and mathematical knowledge of measurable objects and physical forces has a focused and powerful beam, but it is limited in both its range and its penetration as regards reality itself.

Kierkegaard was interested in ultimate truth, and truth of a very personally interested nature: how to live one's life in a true relation to that which is ultimately meaningful and good. It was clear to Kierkegaard that scientific knowledge would not help him in this quest. In the early- to mid-nineteenth century, when Kierkegaard lived, there was a powerful desire to define philosophy and theology in scientific terms. The quest to gain some sort of objective and decisively demonstrated knowledge of ultimate truth was in high dudgeon. Kierkegaard fiercely opposed this trend. This led him to think very deeply about human subjectivity and its relation to meaningful truth.

In his endeavor to hone the quest for meaning in his life, so that the terms of the search were appropriate to the thing being searched for, Kierkegaard coined the word "existential." You should not be frightened by this word for it has a very simple meaning. Kierkegaard maintains that when we try and make sense of the value and meaning of the world, we should start with the personal experiences of our own *existence*, rather than with grand-sounding yet abstract theories about universal objective truth. To Kierkegaard, the love, rivalry, wonder, anxiety, and all those mundane yet richly meaning-laden experiences of our own particular life, constitute the true texture of our actual existence. It seemed obvious to Kierkegaard that we should start searching for meaningful truth from "where" we actually exist.

Inverting Locke, Kierkegaard goes so far as to argue that we must treat subjectively experienced, meaningful concerns as the *primary* concerns of truth, and objective-truth concerns—while important in their own way—as *secondary*. Kierkegaard was well aware that for a number of reasons, making science a secondary-truth discourse is a very *hard* thing for us to do now. We are proud of our objective and functionally materialist realism because of the theoretical and technological jewels it has given us in the scientific age. Further, we have told ourselves that we are advanced in comparison to other times and civilizations, largely because we are scientific, secular, and modern. So it is one of the stunning cultural achievements of modernity that we have trained ourselves to think of the world of objective material things as primary reality, and our interested and personal experience of the value and meanings of things as secondary and merely subjective interpretations. From Kierkegaard's viewpoint, we have got the importance of things exactly the wrong way around.

What is interesting about Kierkegaard is that he explicitly treats our subjective experiences of value, meaning, and transcendence as the arena of the really important and concrete truths of our existence. Detached objectivity is fine for secondary or merely useful matters that don't mean a lot to us, but to Kierkegaard such objectivity is seriously problematic if it displaces our deeply interested and personal concern with truth.

To Kierkegaard, merely systematic factual knowledge is always somewhat abstract, approximate, and—by its very nature—irrelevant to existentially important truth. This does not mean that facts like my faithfulness to my wife are unimportant, but the meaning, context, and interpretation of that fact is what gives that fact its *real* significance. This doesn't mean that the curing of diseases with medical science and the flying of planes with aerophysics are not grounded in objective truth and are not of wonderful utility. It is just that the more important truths of the meaning of a life and the purpose of a trip are not revealed in the knowledge of how one heals and travels.

If we become infatuated with our science and technology to the point where we think they will answer the big existential questions of life, we will live distressingly meaningless lives; for our science of objective things cannot answer our important existential questions of meaning. Worse, if we fail to even ask questions of ultimate meaning because we are relentlessly busy acquiring objective knowledge and instrumental power, we will live sub-human lives. To Kierkegaard, one of the greatest tragedies of his times was that it seemed almost normal for people to be frenetically engaged in the competitive pursuit of measurable power and social status satisfactions, simply because these pursuits are all that is visible to modern objective realism. Kierkegaard found it shocking that the inward and upward quest for existential meaning itself was being displaced by the false priority of the objective over the subjective. This, Kierkegaard thought, would produce a range of despairing social pathologies that would be deeply destructive of meaningful human life. For to Kierkegaard, the challenge of being human is tied up with recognizing and addressing the deep and abiding questions of meaning, value, and transcendence that modern objective truth is entirely blind to.

Kierkegaard developed a way of speaking about this situation that, at first glance, seems shocking. I remember being seriously affronted by my first contact with Kierkegaard and I only read him further in order to prove to myself that he was wrong. (This didn't work, by the way—reading good philosophers is always a risky enterprise.) Kierkegaard's choice of phrase is designed to ruffle and provoke the ideology of modern objectivity. But try not to dismiss his understanding reflexively.

Kierkegaard explains that objectivity is an *existentially* false abstraction if treated as a primary truth discourse. In contrast, then, "truth is subjectivity" as regards our actual experience of the world.[3] But Kierkegaard does not mean by this that the world of

---

3. Kierkegaard's hard reading and masterful text on this topic is his *Concluding Unscientific Post-Script to the Philosophical Fragments*. I would not

physical objects does not exist and that any old subjective meaning is true; not at all. Kierkegaard is keenly aware of how subjectivity is prone to many forms of untruth. He does not even mean that the only access we have to the world of sensible objects is subjective, something we experience inside our heads. No. What he means is that an objective attitude towards detached facts and instrumental effectiveness—the so called realism of a *natura pura* metaphysics—cannot be a true vision of human and cosmic reality if we carefully consider the nature of our actual existence.

Kierkegaard was a modern man of the urban world; he was no medieval mystic. But he noticed *where* magic had shifted to under the conditions of modernity, and he follows that movement from objectivity to subjectivity. Subjectivity—reflective inwardness—has always been the primary existential medium for endeavoring to understand the meaning of our own experience of reality. To take subjective truth seriously is to recognize that the meaning of our life and the world in which we live is not a secondary constructed gloss on a meaningless world of objects. Our actual experience of existence—should we carefully and honestly look—does not match a *natura pura* objectivist ideology.

Kierkegaard's understanding of the truth of subjectivity is much richer than views of reality where sensory facts, or mathematical principles, or logical constructs of pure or ideal reason, are treated as pathways to the real truth about reality. For this reason Kierkegaard delighted in showing up the dead ends and existential follies of modern empiricism, rationalism, and idealism. And, philosophically, these dead ends really are there. Kierkegaard has no problem with paradox and un-provability as such, but the impossible attempt to remove mystery and to bottle the meaning of reality in the terms of what our limited knowledge and reason can master, strikes Kierkegaard as a hopeless and existentially

---

suggest you start reading Kierkegaard here though. For a wonderful introduction to Kierkegaard, see Gardiner, *Kierkegaard: A Very Short Introduction*, particularly his chapter 5, "Truth and Subjectivity." Another excellent introduction to Kierkegaard is Simpson, *The Truth Is the Way*.

unrealistic enterprise. We are imposing the categories of objectivity where they simply do not apply.

Subjectivity remains an open way to the truth of the magical, as experienced in our deeply personal encounters with the questions of the meaning of our own lives, and the meaning of the reality in which we actually find ourselves. There are powerful existential reasons to hold that the enchantment we find in our subjective experiences of beauty, love, goodness, etc., is a real enchantment. For—just look and see—the existential context of our actual lives is saturated in wonder, mythic meanings, and the vibrant colors of expansive significance that the black-and-white data of objective facts simply cannot see. Our existential subjectivity remains a world alive with rich meanings, values, and high longings that objective disenchantment cannot obliterate.

And then there is imagination.

IMAGINATION AND ENCHANTMENT

Imagination was always treated more seriously in the two premodern theories of magic than it is in the two modern theories of magic. There are interesting reasons for this. When it is taken as given that magic is in the natural world (whether only in, or both in and beyond) then it is expected that there will be layers to our understanding. There will be things that we "stand over" and things that we "under stand"; things that are the grounds of our ability to know, and things that we know with that ability. William Desmond—a beautiful contemporary Irish philosopher—is a thinker who employs this sort of outlook today.[4] Here, the dependable habits of natural things and forces can be "stood over" with our experimental and mathematical knowledge, but the meaning of nature is something we "understand" in an open and imaginative way; a way open to transcendence that most appropriately calls a poetic response from us. It is for this reason that myth, poetry, dance, art, and music were deeply integral to all higher

4. See Desmond, *The Intimate Strangeness of Being.*

truth outlooks until modernity. Desmond shows us how Celtic existential lyricism and very sharp logical and scientific thinking can be natural partners, even today. But all this is dispensed with if we assume that nature is purely natural, and particularly so if we have a supernaturalist view of our own mind. This, actually, is what René Descartes—the great French inventor of the modern scientific method—did.

To Descartes, the human mind is a supernatural, non-extended, thinking entity that is (somehow) connected to the physical machine of the human body. This mind-directed human body-machine moves around in the physical objectivity of the purely material world. I cannot resist noting what a fantastic mythic construct of the human imagination this vision of ourselves and the world is. Be that as it may, the modern world largely believes this myth and experiences the world through its interpretive lens.

Here our minds are supernaturally superior to every natural thing, all natural things are inert and merely material objects, and freedom, will, value, purpose, and meaning reside in our (supernatural) minds alone. This outlook enables us to pursue metaphysically and religiously unhindered manipulative power over nature. By seeing nature as a huge matrix of contingent mechanical relations of exchange between material objects, forces, and information, all embedded in a mathematical set of operational laws, we have indeed gained controlling mastery over many natural things that, prior to the scientific revolution, mastered us. Ironically, by science we have become magicians standing over nature and bending it to our own will. But this magical power comes at the cost of divorcing subjective human meanings from objective natural things. And this makes subjectivity and imagination false when they are thought of as projecting human meanings and values onto the natural world. Imagination has been excised from natural reality and sundered from truth. This sacrifice is the cost paid in order to gain our modern powers.

But . . . what if nature really is full of magic? What if our imaginative and lyrical powers are also a part of nature, and the most appropriate part of nature for touching its high mysteries?

The origin of the Harry Potter phenomenon is a little pub in Oxford where a small group of scholarly friends met to workshop the imagination. This group was called The Inklings and C. S. Lewis and J. R. R. Tolkien were two of its members. The unifying principle on which they all agreed was that, for us humans, imagination is the most basic carrier of truth. They were all highly educated thinkers with a deep familiarity with different fields of pre-modern literature, culture, and knowledge, so they noticed how historically strange the transcendence-denying "realism" in British philosophy circles was in the mid-twentieth century. People like Bertrand Russell, A. J. Ayer, and exports to the colonies such as John Anderson, promoted something of an atheist religion of scientific logic, free love, and social progress. To this outlook only matter and energy are real. All human meanings, morals, and values are thus only valid to the extent that they are hedonistic interpretive glosses on a spiritless and entirely material cosmos. The Inklings thought that the problem with the worldview of reductive materialism was its impoverished imaginative landscape, such that it actually gave a false view of reality. Their response to this situation was to seek to reawaken the imagination to truth, not by trying to argue about truth with people who only saw truth in materialist terms, but by telling good stories. In many regards, this strategy worked.

Early in the twentieth century, Bertrand Russell was at the spearhead of a British push back against a deep Continental interest in myth, interpretation, and idealist speculations about Spirit and "the Absolute." At this time, Nietzsche's understanding of the imaginative and mythic foundations of knowledge, power, and meaning had produced a lasting impact on Continental thought. This Continental outlook influenced the French and German leaders in the emerging social and psychological sciences. But Russell largely stamped out the British idealists who had sought to connect Continental trajectories with the British academy.[5]

---

5. A fascinating account of the demise of British idealism and the rise of scientistic reductionism is outlined in Collingwood, *An Autobiography*.

Russell's personal charisma, progressive hedonism, political activism, and powerful logical reasoning contributed much to the influence of twentieth-century British materialism in our universities. This movement contributed significantly to two deep cultural transitions in the English-speaking world. (Ivory tower academics are actually our myth-makers and their sociological influence is never to be underestimated.) Firstly, British materialism sought to remove value, meaning, and morality from both nature and religion. That is, moral truth was neither in nor beyond the world, it only resided in social conventions, which were deemed valid or not only by how they distributed pleasure and pain to the individual and society. This "naturalist" morality is premised on the denial of quality in nature. Instinct and sensation become bereft of meaning in themselves, and pleasure becomes not good in any genuinely qualitative sense, but is simply instinctively preferable to pain. It is a naturalism where sensation and instinct are glossed with meaning, but have no meaning in themselves, other than as Darwinian sub-rational drives for survival or propagation. James Franklin convincingly traces a social history of this progressive movement from the 1920s to the 1960s in Australian universities.[6] Sexual individualism liberated young people from traditional familial norms defined by conventionally "natural" or religious custom in the 1960s such that familial norms have been profoundly re-defined since that time. Secondly, while public figures like Russell did have excellent utilitarian reasons for opposing nuclear war in the 1950s, if there is no moral reality to nature itself, then an irrational "realism" of aggressive military brinkmanship is just as instinctively natural as utilitarian peace. That is, winning a nuclear arms race or pursuing a utilitarian conception of world peace are not *morally* distinguishable, they are only *preferentially* distinguishable within an overarching amoral naturalism. Ironically, treating morality as an entirely human construct gave potent support to a "realist" politics of instrumental and violent force, facilitated by modern science. For the will to domination and destruction is, after all, just as natural and strong as (if not stronger than) the

6. Franklin, *Corrupting the Youth: A History of Philosophy in Australia.*

will to peace and pleasure. The twentieth century saw previously undreamt of military technologies and applications that could be placed at the disposal of this amoral naturalistic "realism." British materialist appropriations of the scientistic myth of progress, tied in with a supposedly biological understanding of the upward surge of competitive domination instincts, had a deep impact on the way we saw ourselves and nature in the twentieth century. Ironically, this is a powerful imaginative mythos, but it is one that despises myth and religion, and that is dogmatically committed to the anti-magical theory of magic. This bleak and violent imaginative image of reality is what the Inklings sought to counter via fantasy, via the imagination.

We now find ourselves in the position where existential philosophers (like Kierkegaard) and hermeneutic philosophers (people who think hard about the nature of human meaning) grasp the primary truth-carrying nature of human subjectivity. Further, thinkers after Nietzsche understand the foundational role of myth in the way we actually frame a coherent outlook on reality, which embeds our collective truth-frameworks unavoidably and deeply in imagination. These insights are well grasped by our sociological thinkers, particularly as influenced by Continental thinking. But culturally, a Russellite ideology of disenchanted objective truth, and of an entirely instinctive and constructed understanding of human meaning, deeply shapes our lifeworld.

Something much bigger than a science-versus-religion war is going on here. That sort of conflict thesis is something of an internal dispute between the two modern theories of magic about whether pure nature is all there is, or whether pure nature is in some manner accompanied by a non-sensible supernature. What we are really looking at is a very uneasy stalemate between the two modern theories of magic in the realm of objectivity, and the two ancient theories of magic in the realm of subjectivity. This is a decidedly uncomfortable peace because the realm of objectivity can only be divided from the realm of subjectivity in an artificial and carefully policed manner. For in reality, we are integral beings and objectivity and subjectivity deeply interact with each other all the time.[7]

One thing is clear: in all of these frames of objective knowledge and subjective meaning, mythos and imagination are profoundly active. So the only thing that can be stated for sure about this situation is that the myth of disenchantment—taken as a flat realist truth—is deeply dishonest and not finally viable. Disenchantment never actually happened, nor is it possible.

7. See Latour, *We Have Never Been Modern.*

THE MAGIC OF QUALITY
AND PURPOSE

Kierkegaard maintains that the truths of meaning and value are among the primary and most important realities of our actual existence. Kierkegaard makes a powerful case that we have good existential reasons to treat our experience of quality and meaning as real. These are, after all, obvious and profoundly important features of our daily lives. The existential experiences we will explore in this lesson are the aesthetic quality of beauty, the moral quality of goodness, and the meaning category of purpose. We will seek to establish whether we can credibly believe that these sorts of non-scientific qualities are real.

First up, I need to clarify what quality and purpose are *not*, as we actually experience them. We do not encounter quality as a cultural fiction tacked onto our materialist and instrumental experience. In practice, we do *not* make a "good" choice by quantifying and mechanizing all data and relation inputs, subjecting them to an objective cost–benefit calculation, and then rationally weighing various instrumental pathways that would maximize our own interest. We may rationalize value *afterwards* in this way, and perhaps value might really be of this nature; but that is not how (as far as I know) anyone actually *experiences* good qualities and intrinsic purposes, such as beauty and goodness. As we experience value, it is genuinely qualitative, which is to say, it cannot be quantified and measured, and we do not experience it as coming from within us, but as being inspired by the world. The value of beauty—such as a breath-taking sunset—cannot be quantified. No intrinsic value—such as loyalty to a friend—can be sold or bought. No genuine love is simply about how the lover egotistically feels and desires. These are unavoidable and foundational truths of our lived experience.

Likewise, we do not experience purpose as reducible to what is beneficial for survival or the enhancement of power. Survival and power are not, in themselves, meaningful purposes. As we experience it, survival and power are *means* to living a meaningful and purposive life, but they are not the *end* of a meaningful and purposive life. If we have meaningful ends that we aim at, then we can act and plan with purpose so as to organize our life in such a way that we are realizing valuable ends. A valuable end is something that is valuable not as a means to something else, but for its own, genuinely qualitative sake. That is, the *quality of goodness* defines a meaningful and valuable end. A good life is purposive and meaningful, whether it survives for a long or short time, and whether it has expansive powers at its disposal, or very limited powers at its disposal.

You can probably see where I am going by setting up our experience of value and purpose in this way. For value and purpose understood in the actual categories of our existential experience are magical to the terms of modern realism. This is because modern realism only counts what you can materially observe, quantifiably measure, and then mathematically model as real. This means we modern people are required to *reinterpret* our direct (magical) experience of value and purpose in the abstract (so-called "realist") terms of quantification and instrumental function. Thus, biological necessity and social conditioning become the primary realities of human motivation (for these things are materially measurable) and quality becomes a secondary and subjective fiction produced by "real" material causes.

It is a fascinating feature of our modern cultural development that we have increasingly tried to define instinct itself as good, as if meaningful motivation could be fully defined by purely natural attractive and repulsive instincts. In contrast, outlooks that treat quality and purpose as features of reality have always treated natural fears and desires as capable of right sympathetic alignment with goodness, and also as capable of antagonistic opposition to goodness. For example, to Shakespeare, instincts were never simply good or bad because they were natural. This is because the qualitative was thought of as a real and primary feature of nature, and nature itself was not reducible to merely quantifiable material categories.

Now maybe it is really true that value and purpose—in their own terms—do not exist. Certainly it is possible to observe human behavior and analyze people's motivations in quantified, instinct-motivated, utility-maximizing, rationalization terms. Obviously, useful manipulative techniques for modifying human behavior via the use of this sort of analysis can be produced. This modern "realist" approach to value and purpose obviously "works," or else psychiatry and advertising would not work. So if effective instrumental power is the same thing as truth, then values and purposes are indeed not real in the terms of value and purpose. However, even though "quantities" of pleasure and pain, genetics, herd conditioning, etc., are indeed integral to our experience of quality and purpose, that in itself does not establish whether quality and purpose can be meaningfully *reduced* to a *natura pura* analysis of the physical context in which we experience them.

Modern materialist reductionism is undoubtedly instrumentally powerful, but that, in itself, does not make it true. In other words, "knowledge is power" is only true in relation to manipulative knowledge, but such knowledge has no necessary relation to qualitative truth. This, when we think about magic, must be insisted on. For it is our commitments to a *natura pura*, disenchanted model of *knowledge* that makes it necessary for us to interpret value as if it is not real in the terms in which it is experienced.

Within modern knowledge our entire discourse of factual truth is embedded in one or other of the modern theories of magic, and both of these theories of magic are strongly opposed to the existence of magic in nature and in our direct experience of the world. Through the social conditioning of modern knowledge, the question of whether a reductively physical conception of value is true or not—or even makes any sort of sense—does not even arise for us when we are thinking in terms of "hard facts."

As previously mentioned, subjective beliefs, fantasies, and the realm of qualitative and purposive experience are immediately and centrally important to our actual lives. So subjectivity and imagination are naturally taken very seriously by us, existentially. The strange thing, though, is the way we cannot take all these vitally important existential matters as being genuinely real in their own terms. For under the assumptions of *natura pura* reality, we isolate "real" *objective* things from "constructed" *subjective* meanings. We really cannot integrate knowledge and wisdom, facts and meanings, truth and quality, instrumental power and morality, beauty and science, technology and goodness, . . . faith (and here I just mean good faith in a meaningful and qualitative cosmos) and reason.

The most significant carrier of the existential categories of quality and purpose is love. Let us think about love and magic.

THE MAGIC OF LOVE

Annette (my spouse) and I have four daughters. I appreciate that not everyone lives in a loving family and that there really are other ways of having a deeply valuable and purposive life. But to me, the love I give and receive in my family gives value and purpose to my life that is very significant and deeply integral with my sense of living a good and meaningful life. Certainly there were instinctive powers strongly at work in the erotic attraction that awakened me to even think of getting married and having a family, and powerful paternal instincts are embedded in the way I experience being a father. But after twenty-five years of being married I can assure you

that Annette and I have been through more than one serious tragedy and many trials and sufferings that we would not have experienced if we had not got married and had children. This does not
make love a bad idea: indeed the deep flowering of love over time
is a discovery about the higher goods of self-giving love, and these
higher goods are what the immature, self-gratifying, early infatua-
tions of love have always pointed to. Conversely put, if love was *really* just about sex and passing on one's genes, then every married
life is a needless and instinctively unaccountable drudgery.

As a thought experiment, let us imagine that instead of mar-
rying Annette twenty-five years ago, I had opted rather for the
non-committal life of short-term "adult" relationships—and no
children—while career ambition and my own financial success
were my first love. I would have had decidedly more "freedom,"
decidedly less responsibility than I have, I could have been much
more self-indulgent, and I would not have experienced the deep
sufferings of love. However, common wisdom would judge that
such a life would have been less valuable and less purposive, precisely because I did not chose the commitments of love. It would
have been more "reasonable"—in a merely hedonistic and calcula-
tive way—and more "natural"—in a merely instinct-defined way,
to not get married. But how wise would that sort of reasoning and
supposed naturalness really have been? If I had valued freedom,
power, sex, and money more than the long and suffering labors of
love, by any measure of wisdom, I would have been a fool. This is a
basic truth in the West's wisdom heritage. As the Song of Solomon
puts it: "If one were to give all the wealth of one's house for love, it
would be utterly despised."

To wisdom, love is not a quantifiable and saleable commod-
ity. Love is not an experience or possession one can instrumentally
use for the sake of some more pressing and important purpose.
Love is valuable *for itself*, and the life guided by purposes that serve
love is a life that is intrinsically meaningful. But, of course, love
is much bigger than marriage. Marriage—to the West's religious
traditions—is an important sacrament of love, but there are many
sacraments of love. Indeed, many of the greatest poets, artists,

philanthropists, and saints are convinced that Love is the deep magic in which the very cosmos is embedded.

This brings us back to magic; deep magic. This, after all, is what C. S. Lewis in his Narnia stories was really writing about. He was writing about a cosmic metaphysics of love. Tolkien also writes out of that metaphysics. Further, they haven't just made this up. It is the metaphysics of Augustine and Dante, Chaucer and Shakespeare, Bach and Rachmaninov, Hopkins and Chesterton. It is the metaphysics of J. K. Rowling. Are we going to say that the deep magic of the metaphysics of love is merely an entertaining fantasy? Are we going to presume that, *really*, love is an internal interpretive gloss on the meaningless facts of material objects and socio-biological necessity?

Of course, there are alternative metaphysical visions of the first reality of the cosmos to love. There is a metaphysics of power and will in perpetual struggle with chaos. This is a vision where domination and the relentless struggle to survive define the good—or at least successful—life. And of course, the texture of reality is very rich and varied, and no one metaphysical story seems fully adequate to make sense of all the deep things of our experience. In any deep picture of reality there is always a place for what theologians call "the cloud of unknowing."

But what difference would it make if we, collectively, were to think one thing or another about qualitative metaphysics?

QUALITATIVE METAPHYSICS

Actually, there are very few things more practically and socially significant than one's culture's assumed metaphysics. If we live in a life-world shaped by the metaphysics of *natura pura*, which proclaims that instinct and material needs are what really motivates all human action, this will profoundly shape the way we do economics and politics. Neoliberal political economics, for example, maintains that the personal freedom to pursue materially defined self-interest is the obvious "good" that polities and markets should deliver to individuals. Here fear and greed are the obvious real drivers of the market, and are "good" because they are natural. Given a first-reality vision of struggle, we find that a *morality* of fear and greed, focused around personal freedom, is imposed on us by our collective way of life. To this outlook, being rich, powerful, and secure is to have achieved the good life, and so the poor, the weak, and the insecure are increasingly viewed as morally defective. We are producing a life-world defined by a metaphysics of cosmic struggle, which glorifies the *libido dominandi*—the lust for power—of our elites.

We make the social reality of our way of life real by practicing the values and meanings consistent with the knowledge and power structures of our society. (As Bruno Latour has noticed, facts and meanings actually *are* integrated in real life.) But this does not make all social life-forms equal. Unless, that is, nature really has no meaning and value. But look what happens here. If all values and meanings are made up by us, then surely we could make up a system of morality and power than did not rely on the exploitation and insecurity of the many for the sake of the wealth and power of the few? Indeed, would it not be inevitable that the majority would make this happen in pursuit of their own best interests? This was certainly how Karl Marx saw things.

In the mid-twentieth century, Marxism was a global ideological power pushing for radical egalitarianism. This outlook was opposed by an ideology of personal freedom allowing elitism and Christianity as promoted by the US during the Cold War. Interestingly, what these ideological opponents had in common was a modern "realist" view of power premised on a residually supernaturalist capitalist stance in the US, and an anti-magic communist stance in the USSR. Both ideologies were embedded in a modern "pure nature" outlook, so both had a functionally materialist, "realist" outlook on power, and both lacked any practical qualitative metaphysics. What metaphysics of love the capitalist West did have was neatly cordoned off from nature and practical public action, and safely tucked away in heaven, the private home, and subjective feelings. What metaphysics of camaraderie in class warfare the communist world had, degenerated into a brutal herd conformity, as was only natural given a very naturalist view of power. Neither view could even consider whether nature itself has any magical qualitative and purposive reality that might be expressed in what the pre-moderns called the *summum bonum*.[1] The idea that there really is quality in nature such that the morality and justice of our wealth and power structures is not simply something we make up for ourselves, is not available to the two modern theories of magic or the political ideologies that arise from them. For our "realist" view of power is functionally defined by a "pure nature" of quantities, forces, and meaningless matter alone.

Perhaps our poets, novelists, and fantasy writers—embedding love and value in reality—are being truer to reality than political ideologies embedded in modern visions of pure nature allow? Perhaps matter itself is meaningful? Perhaps there is a deep interchangeability between matter, energy, mind, purpose, and value? Perhaps, even, God is love, and there is a transcendent basis to a metaphysics of love that includes both freedom and equality within it, that we cannot find if we set either freedom or equality up as the first idols of our political ideologies? I cannot pretend to even start to answer any of these questions in this little book on magic, but I can say that these are very important questions to ask. I can also say that it is entirely reasonable to ask them, if one is not determined to be anti-magical or supernatural on the basis of a dogmatic faith commitment to a modern *natura pura* metaphysics.

Value and purpose are qualitative realities of prime importance in our actual lives. These magical realities are outside of the reality landscape of modern pure nature, but they have not disappeared just because we have become modern. A metaphysics of love is deeply integral with our Western cultural heritage, and we would not have the hospitals, fire services, public education, legal and political rights, etc., that we do have if it was not for this heritage. The eighteenth-century movement for the abolition of slavery

---

1. In classical and medieval thinking, the *summum bonum* is the highest good, the good that defines whether a political economic order is itself imaginatively aligned with a true metaphysics of value, or not.

would not have succeeded in the nineteenth century without the appeal to a metaphysics of divine love, embedded in the human world via the *imago Dei*. The concept of universal human rights is a twentieth-century restatement of those same abolitionist metaphysical convictions by Eleanor Roosevelt, though globally universalized beyond the Christian religion. Undergirding the kind and humane concept of intrinsic human dignity—for humanists of all or no religious persuasion—is the commitment to the reality of value and meaning that is invisible to a pure nature metaphysics of mere objects and their necessary attractive and repulsive relations. The magic of value and meaning has not gone away; this magic remains a deep definer of our social, moral, and political norms.

LESSON SIX

THE MAGIC OF ESSENCE

If you recall, we have four theories of magic situated within two broad understandings of nature. We have ancient animist and Platonist theories embedded in enchanted understandings of nature, and we have modern supernatural and anti-magic theories embedded in disenchanted understandings of nature. As pointed out, magic has not gone away just because we have become modern. Value and meaning still define what is most important in our lives, even though these things have no natural reality, *as* value and meaning, within the *natura pura* conceptual universe. This begs an obvious question: is our modern experience of value and meaning a deluded fiction, or is our modern conception of a *natura pura* cosmos a deluded fiction? In order to try and get somewhere with this question, this lesson will run each of our four theories through a test. We will test them on essence.

Essence is intimately entailed in the notion of a cosmos characterized by meaningful intelligibility. I will here quickly outline the basic premodern conception of essence. I need to explain this to you because essence is a concept that has become increasingly incomprehensible within modern *natura pura* realism, as well as postmodern *natura pura* constructivism. Modern and post-modern stances offer alternatives to essence, and we will look at them and think about magic in the light of them. But the basic pre-modern idea of essence is a beautifully elegant and naturally persuasive idea.

Now I am aware that an essence test is not neutral as regards these four theories of magic. Indeed, essence is a concept that lives only within an enchanted nature. But the reason why I am going to run them all through essence will become clear as we go, and I will find ways of being reasonably fair to the two modern theories of magic in this process. At least, that is my intention.

Essence in premodern thinking was tied up with both be-ing (ontology) and knowing (epistemology). In ancient times there was an enormous variety of pre-classical speculative theories about the nature and knowledge of the world, and in the time of Plato and Aristotle, things largely settled out into two broad schools of epistemology. On the one hand, there was a skeptical trajectory. Here truth cannot really be known and the cosmos can only be thought of as a rationally integrated unity by means of an act of projective fiction, which may be more or less useful than treating "it" as simply unintelligible. To be clear, ancient skepticism has some really brilliant thinkers among its ranks, and although it fell into near total abeyance after the collapse of the classical civilization, it makes a stunning recovery in Western intellectual history (not coincidentally) in the seventeenth and eighteenth centuries. This trajectory rejects the idea of essence. The other trajectory embraces the idea of essence.

Both Plato and Aristotle thought that we can know the world because all beings in the world have an intellective essence, a "form." That is, it is in the nature of a being to have defining qualities and characteristics, and it is in the nature of the world that it is an intellectively integrated and logical cosmos where all individual beings are unified through Being itself.

When we know something, we grasp something of its essence in our mind. Now we may only ever have a partial knowledge of the true essence of things, and we certainly have a very limited knowledge of Being, and even less of its divine grounds, but what truth we can grasp is genuine truth. Here, the essential nature of all things is fundamentally communicative and fundamentally intellective. So *Being* conceived of as in some manner the divinely given framework of reality; *Logos* as the ordered communicative reason expressed in all aspects of the cosmos; and *form* or *essence*, giving specific knowable characteristics to beings in the world, all conspire to make the world intelligible to us. Here, the cosmos itself is embedded in Mind (*Nous*), and our minds are in communion with the cosmos-ordering Mind that is the ground of being and that defines the field of reality. To the essentialist stream of classical and medieval thinking, thought is meaningful and knowledge can be true because *the nature of reality itself is intrinsically intellective.* (Let that sink in . . . there is a lot in that sentence.)

The difficult thing to explain in this outlook was not mind (this is the difficulty for the modern materialist) but matter. Aristotle tried to integrate aspects of the high essentialism of the Platonist trajectory with the materialist thinking of Democritus, and came up with the idea that matter is the medium of form, such that there is no form without it being expressed in matter and no matter that is not in-formed with reasoned intellective essence. As briefly indicated back in lesson three, medieval difficulties with what an unformed medium of form (prime matter), in itself, could actually be, contributed to the serious unravelling of medieval Aristotelian metaphysics, but that need not concern us here.

To classical and medieval epistemology and metaphysics, Mind was the most basic feature of reality, and all material beings (as well as immaterial beings) were embedded in thought. Anyone who did not take this as the *premise* of reasoning was not serious about reason itself, and you would be wasting your time if you tried to reason with them. Thus, those skeptics who were not prepared to have good faith in reason itself could be relied on to play sophistic linguistic tricks in conversation, and to substitute irrational desire or power or pleasure for reason as the basic ground of human communication and action. This entails an irrational and instrumental fatalism that both Plato and Aristotle and their many types of followers found beneath philosophical reasonableness. For the truth possibilities of reasonable speech were—to the essentialists—all premised on the cosmos being produced and enchanted by divine Mind. In this cosmos, value, purpose, beauty, unity, meaning, and goodness were all real features of *natural* reality, as well as human reality. In this cosmos, a reasonable knowledge of the world is entirely natural, and the world itself is embedded in the higher values and meanings of Mind.

What I want you to notice here is that divine Mind—which is also, to Plato, the ground of Being, and the Goodness beyond Being—is the ontological foundation of knowledge to this outlook. That is, a vision of reality as intrinsically ordered, intrinsically meaningful, intrinsically valuable *is the ground* of our sense experience, and of all human meaning, purpose, reason, and knowledge.[1] Nature (as far as we are concerned) is here a medium of communication between the divine Mind and human minds, and we are ourselves situated within this shimmering, beautiful, and yet unmasterable and inherently mysterious, meaningful medium (nature). The intellective essence of any being or thought we experience has its first source in the Mind of God, and when we comprehend any intellectual truth, we are hearing the Logos of God speak into our minds.

As a quick aside, I should point out that one does not need to be religious to think about the meaning of the cosmos along these sort of lines. Professor Paul Davies—see his book *The Mind of God*—is a physicist and entirely non-religious, and yet the intellectually brilliant structures and the delicately balanced and beautifully elegant synergies of nature leads Davies to think about reality in ways that have quite serious ties to this ancient essentialist outlook.[2]

We have seen that the notion of essence is actually part of a wider theory of intelligibility and cosmic meaning. As is obvious, the Platonist theory of magic is fully aligned with this theory of cosmic and human intelligibility. The animist theory is problematically aligned with it as the medium of Nature is also the Mind that speaks through the medium. The supernatural theory is related to

1. See Gerson, *Ancient Epistemology*.
2. Davies, *The Mind of God*.

54

the Platonist theory, in that there is a divine Mind beyond nature that donates meaning and order to nature, and yet that divinity seems so separated from nature that nature cannot be treated as a medium of divine communication. To the supernaturalist the intelligibility of nature becomes reduced to a function of the will and intentions of our own supernatural minds, tending towards treating nature as a mechanistic thing with no inherent meaning or value. To the anti-magical outlook, our minds become purely physical, and inherently meaningless and valueless. Here our intellections must be a strange epiphenomena of matter, within pure materiality. For these reasons modern magical theories cannot appropriate essentialist understandings of intellection. But here is the question: what is a sensible way of thinking about the intelligible, meaningful, and valuable nature of nature?

Let us pair theories differently in an attempt to answer this question. Let us put Platonist and supernatural theories together as different theories of divine communication that explain the intelligibility of nature; let as put animist and anti-magical theories together as approaches to intelligibility that are either intra-cosmic (within Nature) or epiphenomenal properties of matter, that require no Mind beyond nature.

To animism and anti-magic first.

The final lesson of Professor Carlo Rovelli's beautiful little book on physics seeks to tentatively synthesize aspects of ancient semi-animist and skeptical naturalism with modern anti-magical naturalism.[3] Rovelli is not an animist in the manner of ancient peoples who worship spirits of the land, animals, heavens, and ancestors, where Nature is itself divine. Even so, Rovelli is a close reader of Anaximander and Lucretius, who were ancient Greco-Roman naturalists that did have closer ties with ancient animism than is possible for a modern thinker. But we will leave strong animism to one side here, even though it should be taken seriously as possibly the most ancient and natural theory of magic within the history of the human condition. But here, I wish to use (hopefully not too unfairly) Rovelli as a contemporary advocate of a blending

3. Rovelli, *Seven Brief Lessons on Physics*, 63–79.

of anti-magical and skeptical modern scientism with a more reverential and haunted ancient naturalism. For Rovelli, as a scientist, is looking for a way of seeing the magic of nature, and grasping the *meaning* of ourselves as part of nature. This is a stance that can work, but I will critique this stance before returning to its ongoing viability.

Here, as I see it, is Rovelli's problem. After the modern fashion, Rovelli sees our knowledge as foundational for whatever meaning and value we can read from nature. This is an entirely modern move because our minds stand over a reductively material nature, and the only locus of interpretive and intellective meaning in reality that we can naturally know is within our minds. So the cosmos may or may not be inherently intelligible, may or may not have essential meanings, intrinsic values, and final purposes within it, and there may or may not be any higher reality beyond and beneath material nature, but—to a modern thinker—the only meaning *we* can know is inside our own heads. Modern philosophy is built upon an approach known as "epistemological foundationalism," according to which only what we can know for sure can be a foundation on which a valid understanding of the nature of reality is built.

There are three problems with this. Firstly, epistemological foundationalism has been the bane of modern philosophy. Starting philosophy by seeking certain knowledge simply doesn't work. Secondly, this is a deeply *ontologically pre-determined* approach (due to an assumed *natura pura* cosmology) that is not open and honest about its assumptions concerning reality. Thirdly—and as a consequence of the second point above—as you will only find what you are looking for, if you are after a *natura pura* account of cosmic intelligibility and cannot find it, you are likely to conclude that intelligibility does not really exist in the cosmos and is only epiphenomenally in our own minds. However, such a view of intelligibility undermines the real meaning of all knowledge, language, and intelligence and leads (ironically) to *thinking* of knowledge as merely a means of power, a function of socially and biochemically situated material determinates, or an endlessly re-interpreted field of play. It seems that this last option—Derridean postmodernism—has natural ties to ancient skepticism and animist-tinted mythopoetic naturalism, but it hardly provides a believable theory of intelligibility.

It seems likely that epistemological foundationalism can only lead to the deep unknowing of skepticism and the linguistic maze of pre-Socratic and postmodern sophistry. In other words, an anti-magical modern naturalism can provide no adequate account of the intelligibility of the cosmos. It seems to me that Rovelli—as a scientist in love with the wondrous yet shimmering intelligibility of the natural world, and as a modern materialist who is drawn to the ancient naturalism that borders on animism—wants to have his modern scientific cake and magically eat it too. If nature is really intelligible, then this needs to be understood as a genuine ontological reality rather than as something of an internal interpretive trick of our brains. For if you are not prepared to start from the intelligibility of nature, skeptical knowledge of the perceived world will not provide you with a very convincing pathway to intelligibility.

But perhaps pure matter really is magical. Perhaps—as Rovelli suggests—the mere physical complexity of our brains embodies the quantum marvels of matter, and perhaps mind simply is matter, and matter naturally self-organized in such a way as to produce both consciousness and an intelligible cosmos. This possibility leans much more closely to magical animism than to anti-magical modern materialism. Such an outlook would not actually be compatible with the reductive materialism of modern *natura pura* visions of nature, in which modern science is deeply embedded. Enchanted matter in a magical cosmos has more in common with our actual experience of wonder and meaning in the world than a deflationary materialism of pure nature has, but such a naturalism cannot be so neatly and patronizingly dismissive of the animist, Platonist, and supernatural outlooks as modern anti-magic thinking is. Yet here, the intelligibility of the cosmos does not need essence from a transcendent cosmic Mind. Here our mind and the universe are in obvious sympathy because matter and mind, like matter and energy, are really different modes of the same thing. So Rovelli may indeed have a viable way forward here. But should he go down this path, then he is re-positioning ontology and even theology as the foundation of science, if he is starting from the premise of the meaningful and intelligible nature of nature itself. This would entail quite a profound shift away from *natura pura* theories of both nature and scientific knowledge.

Very briefly, to Platonism.

As outlined above, essence is a Platonist theory of intelligibility. The intelligibility of the world is the foundation of modern science, and this foundation is historically there in modern science as a strangely out of place Platonist carryover into the supernaturalist view of pure nature. Platonist essence remains an inherently viable way of understanding the intelligibility of the world and of ourselves as thinking, understanding, and knowing beings.[4] Whilst no theory of reality has all the answers or fully escapes profound difficulties of one sort or another, the modern fashionable tendency to simply dismiss Platonism is intellectually unwarranted. Plato remains one of the outstandingly great minds of the Western intellectual tradition. If one takes the intelligibility of reality as a defining feature of reality itself, then clearly, a Platonist magic of essence remains a live option.

---

4. As an excellent introduction to Plato, see Howland, *The Republic: The Odyssey of Philosophy*. For a fine example of powerful contemporary Platonist thinking, see Schindler, *Plato's Critique of Impure Reason*.

IS PLATONIST MAGIC REASONABLE, TODAY?

By now it should be pretty clear where my own sympathies about our four theories of magic lie. I think magic is in the world, today, and I also think magic itself (qualitative reality) is not simply immanent within nature, but transcends nature. I am a Platonist.

Before going any further I should say a few brief things about why supernaturalist and anti-magical forms of modern materialism deeply dislike Plato, and all -isms associated (fairly or otherwise) with him.

Because material nature is a medium of divine forms in Plato, the material exists as a secondary order of reality when compared to the intellective (spiritual) realm. To Plato, the realm of the material is quite incomprehensible if one tries to consider it in isolation from the intellective, because all one will see if one looks for an abstracted, "pure" material nature (matter apart from form) is contingency and flux. Things cannot be understood—things would have no enduring essence—if matter and energy in temporal and material transience is all there is. Indeed, there could be no such thing as "things" in such flux. If the limits of our senses and the grammar of our logic are all we have to go on, then the apparent reality we think we perceive and understand cannot be known as true, and is itself a function of incomprehensible flux and contingency. Plato has no interest in such an anti-reason, absurdist stances. To Plato, the things that make material nature really (albeit partially) intelligible are eternal truths. Eternal truths are not subject to contingency and flux. Mathematical truths, for example, are timelessly and essentially true. Through mathematics we see that the material space-time realm of flux and contingence is embedded in the eternal realm of Mind and the eternal "now" of Being. This embedding gives the tangible world its remarkable order, intelligibility, and reality. This divine realm of Mind produces the high forms: Beauty, Being, Unity, Truth, and above all Goodness. Value, meaning, reason, and purpose are found by us within nature because nature itself is embedded in the eternal realm of divine forms. But the point of deep wisdom for Plato is not so much the mastery of the physical world, it is preparation for the life of the soul after it leaves the physical realm of flux and contingency. According to Plato, the day-to-day concerns of our brief and often bewildering mortal lives should not be thought of as ultimately important. The health or sickness of our eternal soul as it sojourns in the mortal world is where ultimate concern should be focused.

If one is a modern supernaturalist—that is, if one believes that nature and supernature are entirely operationally separated from each other—this splits nature and supernature into a type of dualism unknown to Plato. Remember nature is incomprehensible without the divine, for Plato. But viewed through a supernaturalist lens, Plato looks as if he denigrates material nature, and is only interested in the supernatural. Now indeed, Plato had no interest in modern nature, for he thought that the ancient forms of *natura pura* were quite impossible to take seriously. Plato could not believe that nature—or anything—could be intelligible if one treated it in a so-called "purely" natural sense. Equally, Plato had no interest in a modern, entirely separated supernature. To Plato our embodied minds and all material reality exist, so to speak, "within" the divine Mind, which is the ground of all Being, be it the purely intellective and high being of the eternal forms, or all matter-and-form composite beings that exists in a transitory manner within space and time.

So modern supernaturalists (wrongly) think that Plato has no interest in the material world and is only interested in an entirely supernatural heaven. This makes Plato someone who has no practical relevance when it comes to "the real world." But if one moves from supernaturalism to anti-magical materialism, then Plato looks even more offensive. For to this type of modernism, reality is only material, and this material life is the *only* life, so the mundane concerns of mortal life are its highest concerns and all talk of the transcendent is, at best, impossible moonshine, and at worst, an exploitative political opiate. Thus, modernity tends to think of Plato as a body-hating dualist with no interest in or contact with "the real world."

Philosophically speaking, modern prejudices against Plato are largely anachronistic slanders. To see how body-loving and this-world interested Plato is, simply read his dialogue on erotic love, *The Symposium*.[1] But desiring love, to Plato, does indeed have its highest meaning beyond the passions of the body. And the human world of his own beloved Athens is indeed not an ultimate world, though it does participate imperfectly—as do all human worlds—in the divine meaning that gives it its contingent and fragile meanings and its transitory and poetically grasped beauties.

Regardless, then, of modern prejudices, I am not ashamed to be a Platonist, and it remains a very serious philosophical outlook if one is prepared to approach it with a mind that is not closed against it by modern prejudices about matter, supernature, and magic. But can Platonism be viable in the modern world?

To the extent that Platonism is incompatible with a *natura pura* realism, and to the extent that the knowledge and power norms of the modern world are embedded in either supernaturalist or anti-magical theories of magic, Platonism is not compatible with the modern world. However, if Platonism is correct, then the modern world will be trying to cut against the grain of reality with its understanding and practices of knowledge, value, and power.

1. See Osborne, *Eros Unveiled*.

In the end, this will be the undoing of the modern life-world, and Platonism may well provide us with a way of salvaging—no doubt, by reconfiguring—modernity.

There is need for salvaging modernity because the modern life-world is dying at its own hands. The separation of our truly amazing knowledge and power from our actual experience of value, purpose, and (at least for some) transcendence, gives us two very significant reasons to think that the modern life-world will not endure much longer.

Sociologically speaking, all life-worlds have their infant, mature, and often decrepit expressions. Further, all life-worlds die, be that naturally or by violent conquest. We will come back to this because an obvious charge against Platonism is nostalgia for a lost life-world. But, for the moment, the point I want to make is that it is *our* modernity that is on its way out as a sustainable life-world, *now*. For, as stated above, our knowledge and power is separate from our wisdom. Here wisdom is powerless and outside of the truth categories of our knowledge. This makes us very dangerous, both to nature and ourselves.

In a remarkable suspension of linear time—as myths are want to do—it looks like we might well be the legendary civilization of Atlantis. Cataclysmic global climate destabilization combined with billions of insecure people, hawkish "realist" power, and astonishingly destructive military technologies could not only end our life-world, but could wipe humanity from the face of the earth. Science certainly helped get us into this place, but science itself is powerless to save us. It is not the next technological fix that we should pin our hopes for a future on, it is the cultural acquisition of *wisdom* that is our only real hope. But, given how we have separated knowledge from wisdom, are we capable of becoming wise?

The other reason why modernity cannot last long as a life-world is the unsustainable demands it makes on our practical and theoretical beliefs. Somehow we have to believe that our actual experience of value, purpose, and meaning is not really real, and numerical abstractions and amoral power are real. We are required to believe that our actual experience of magic is only a fantasy.

But look! Consider the beauty of light playing on water. Consider the smells, sights, and sounds of the early morning. Look into the eyes of a child. Think about the shimmering wonders and dazzling complexity of the cosmic minutia of quanta. Think about the impossibly maximal distances that are yet communicatively overcome such that a galaxy exists. Ah! The magic of being! Reality is far richer and more dazzling than any fantasy story.

Magic is real. Magic in (and perhaps beyond) nature is deeply real. Our two modern theories of magic, and the modern life-world, push us out of contact with real reality. Though animist and Platonist life-worlds are now dead—and those now gone life-worlds cannot just be pulled out of the historical cupboard—they did not die at their own hands in the manner in which modernity is dying. The cause of their death was violent conquest by our modern life-world. We killed the animist life-world in Australia—a lifeworld that had evolved and flourished for many thousands of years—and we killed our own Platonist life-world in the West. But because animism and Platonism take magic seriously, they provide something deeply viable out of which we might build a *new* life-world.

There are very interesting things going on in broadly animist terms among eco-feminists; there is a growing and serious interest in indigenous epistemologies; there are many varieties of Buddhist-flavored vitalism within environmental activist circles. As a sociologist, it is—I think—genuinely possible that some sort of environmentally wise cultural sensibility might arise out of this, to set sacred limits on the exploitation of nature and people. We certainly need something that can genuinely temper the rapacious global instrumentalism of our financial and military power elites. World heritage listings are not enough. The polar bear and the Great Barrier Reef will not survive the forecast rise in sea temperature over the next mere half century. We need global answers where wisdom disciplines power, and this we cannot currently do in our liberal, secular, financially governed life-world.

There is a lot you can read about and participate in if you are interested in contemporary animist-tinged magic. This is a genuine attempt to produce a life-world-framing alternative to modern theories of magic. So I will say no more on that here. I want, then, to finish this short argument about magic and reality by advocating the merits of Platonism over animism.

Augustine of Hippo lived in the fourth century, at the end of the period of classical Roman civilization. Augustine was a type of Platonist. He analyzed political power in the following way: The thing that unifies a civilization is its first object of love. Augustine thought that in pagan Rome, the first object of love was personal glory. The religious sensibilities of pagan Rome were broadly animist, and the realm of nature and the gods that it worshipped was embedded in a cosmology of fate and struggle. Mortals were often the playthings of the gods of nature and of fate, but the one thing humans could do was face their mortality with defiance. Glory in death was the highest aspiration of Roman civilization. This aspiration was propagated in many ways, not least of which was blood-thirsty Roman entertainment.[2] One could become a man of renown through great courage in the face of mortal danger, and through great feats of power and conquest. In this way—whether in life or in death—one could cheat death and become in some measure immortal in the history of one's people.

Augustine astutely notices the deep connections between a culture's assumed metaphysics and cosmology—which defines its unifying objects of value and meaning—and its practices of power. If you believe reality is embedded in struggle, if you do not believe in any framework of higher love and goodness beyond the theatre of struggle, then you will be violent to both nature (as the Romans—despite their animism—often were) and people. You

---

2. See Ross, *Gifts Glittering and Poisoned: Spectacle, Empire, and Metaphysics*. Ross' book on Augustine's understanding of the spectacle culture of the Roman arena is an amazing read. Ross applies Augustine's analysis to our own spectacle culture as embedded in our contemporary mass media. Ross argues that the underlying cosmologies of struggle, of "natural" (pagan) desire and of glory, remain as deeply influential in the contemporary arena as they were in the Roman arena. The metaphysics of love and the cosmology of original harmony that Augustine sets against the norm of his own day is presented by Ross as highly relevant to our day.

will even valorize violence and treat it as an object of worship, as the civic cultus of Rome certainly did.

In contrast to a metaphysics where nothing ultimately transcends the cycle of birth, struggle, and death, Augustine embraced a Platonist metaphysics of divine love. The alternative to the Roman City of Man was the universal City of God. Here the first object of love is the transcendent God, who is love, the second object of love was one's neighbor, and the obligations of love towards nature were of stewardship accountable to nature's Creator. The cosmology assumed here is of original harmony rather than original violence. Here, violence and conquest are seen as aberrations rather than as norms. And, in the passion of Christ, Augustine claims that divinity receives rather than inflicts violence as a means of bringing life out of death. This is an astonishing inversion of pagan Roman sensibilities.

My point is that even if one finds that animist understandings of magic are decidedly more existentially believable than our modern theories of disenchanted nature, if one defines reality *only* from nature, then one readily finds violence and dominating exploitation to be entirely natural. To this cosmic perspective, violence is naturally valorized, and there is a certain sense of cosmic tragedy in the finality of mortality that drives a civilization in the direction in which pagan Rome was driven. Animism without empire—such as we had in ancient Australia—develops a kind of dynamic stasis, a deeply adaptive harmony between the beauty and ugliness of nature and a way of life defined by deep listening, deep responsiveness, and genuinely sustainable harmony with the fragile and merciless nature of the ancient and environmentally delicate southern continent. But we are all a people of empire now, and we, following ancient Rome, are increasingly moving into a "naturalized" common cosmology of struggle. In this context, the valorizing of military violence grows ever stronger as tensions in the globally destabilized world rise.

The Frenchmen Paul Ricoeur and René Girard were both deeply interested in what happens when you take the religious consciousness of magic, embedded entirely within nature, as your first frame of reference for cosmic meaning.[3] Here, violence, destruction, domination, and totally indifferent power are profoundly natural; they are—in Saint Paul's terms—the elemental principles of the world. Girard and Ricoeur have very interesting things to say about the natural religious consciousness of human experience. That consciousness is deeply animist, and it has no transcendent framework of ultimate goodness above the elemental powers and balances of Nature. The naturalist religious consciousness of humanity is one of an enchanting stasis between good and evil; a harmony of creation and destruction. In the end, it is an amoral cosmos where good and evil are one. Perhaps that is the truth. Yet, perhaps—as both Girard and Ricoeur think—our very "un-natural" yearning for justice and our deep desire for the triumph of good *over* evil speaks to us of the reality of that which is within and yet ultimately beyond nature.

This is where, I think, Platonism betters animism. Animism only has Nature. Nature can teach us terrible things, and as we are part of Nature, our own violence and irrational will-to-power will always be embraced by some aspects of animism. Our powerful collective drive to self-destruction is itself deeply natural. Natural religions end up valorizing the Marduk and the Kali within. There is a very dark face to animism, be it imperial or not.

To conclude.

In this short argument about magic, I have sought to outline what the four basic theories of magic are, and how our two modern theories of magic are deeply problematic. Modern theories of nature (and supernature) make it very hard for us to treat the obvious magic we experience in nature as real. Even so, we still directly experience magic in the values, meanings, and purposes that define our lives. Our deep fascination with magic in fantasy points to a hunger that our knowledge-culture is not addressing. Modern knowledge cannot address our need to understand magic because it is embedded in the two magic theories that produced

3. Girard, *Violence and the Sacred*; Ricoeur, *The Symbolism of Evil*.

modern knowledge and power. This is a genuinely bad situation. For if we don't treat nature with less instrumental dominion and with more reverence for its magic, we are going to irreparably savage the nature upon which we depend.

I think it is entirely reasonable—and indeed, imperative—to see magic as real. Existentially, we cannot help but take the magic of meaning, value, and purpose as the arena of primary human truth. But we isolate non-scientific meaning from factual truth, and we can no longer coherently reason about the truths of non-scientific meaning. This is very problematic. For what we urgently need is to recover a meaningful sense of the truth of value and meaning and the relation of good and purposive truths to scientific knowledge and practical power. This is possibly the most pressing challenge facing us in our age. For we have astonishing instrumental power that has no strong sense of wisdom when it comes to directing our power towards good ends that benefit all. If we can't direct factual knowledge and instrumental power towards genuinely qualitative, meaningful, and common goods—*high* goods—our very success at procuring low goods will be our ruin. We won't rise to this challenge unless we start thinking seriously about the reality and importance of magic.

THANKYOUS

For the production of such a slim little book as this, I have a surprisingly large amount of people to thank. I would like to thank two employers, three funders, two scholars in particular, four friends, my editor, and my family, as all being very important for the existence of this little book.

Professor Peter Harrison is director of the Institute for Advanced Studies in Humanities (IASH, University of Queensland), where I now work. IASH provides the institutional home for the After Science and Religion Project, which I coordinate. That project has attracted top-tier international philosophical theologians, scientists, and historians to try and re-think the way we understand science and religion. This book is a side output from that project. I know a bit about directing research institutes and I couldn't work under a better director. Many thanks Peter.

When I started looking for participants, institutional partners, and funders for the After Science and Religion Project I was the director of the Emmanuel Centre for the Study of Science, Religion, and Society (University of Queensland). I was employed by Professor David Brunckhorst, who was then the principal at Emmanuel College. Sadly, there was an institutional upheaval at Emmanuel College, and a number of us, including myself and David, no longer work there. But by the time of the upheaval my project was already flying. Clearly, without David's strong institutional support, and without his firm belief in the value of my research ambitions, the project would not have got on the runway. Thank you David for being such a wonderful blue-sky thinker and for your encouragement and friendship.

In the very early stages of the After Science and Religion Project, I was telling my father-in-law, Karl Wiethoff, about my plans and my need—as a research center director—to find funders. He said to me, "why don't you ask me for some help?" Very generously, Karl gave a seeding gift to the institute I then directed, and this was very helpful in getting this project flying. Thanks Pop!

Before we had fully secured our major project funder, the Issachar Fund gave us a grant to meet in Cambridge. That was a wonderful initial gathering, and I am very appreciative of the Issachar Fund's practical show of good faith in this project. Kurt Berends, president of the Issachar Fund, has shown keen, practical, and rapid interest in our project. Unfortunately Kurt couldn't join us for the gathering that Issachar funded, but it was great to have Dr. Mike Hamilton from Issachar and John Sharp from the Blankemeyer Foundation come along as observers to that 2018 gathering in Cambridge. Many thanks for your support, Kurt and Mike, and for your interest, John.

At our initial gathering in Cambridge, many fine papers were read, which are now being worked over and complied. They were all amazing, but one paper in particular made a number of pennies drop for me. That was Professor John Milbank's "Religion, Science and Magic." The main conceptual idea organizing this book opened up to me from reading John's paper. The argument in this little book is my own, but the framework of reasoning that makes this book work owes a lot to John. Many thanks, John.

The other scholar to whom this book is particularly indebted is Professor Carlo Rovelli. I have never met or communicated with this wonderful physicist and philosopher, but it was reading his beautifully written book *Seven Brief Lessons on Physics* that gave me a template and stylistic model for this little volume. Professor Rovelli is an outstanding communicator of complex ideas to the non-specialist reader. I have tried to follow his example in this book, but he is a pinnacle communicator so I fear I remain considerably in his shadow. However, if you read this book, good professor, many thanks for your inspiring example.

After our first gathering, the Templeton World Charity Foundation put their generous resources behind our project. Given that our project is attempting to re-think the science and religion space at the level of first principles, supporting this project is a genuinely bold enterprise. I am very grateful to Dr. Peter Jordan for his keen interest in this project and the TWCF for their preparedness to give this trajectory a go. Many thanks Peter and TWCF.

Four friends of mine and my editor at Wipf and Stock—all amazingly thoughtful and creative thinkers—read this manuscript over very carefully: Dr. Spike Bucklow, Dr. Jonathan Horton, Dr. Robin Parry, Yuval Luski, and Dr. Stuart Weierter. I have not been able to follow all of their suggestions and all faults with the text remain my own, but the wonderful advice of these friends has been very helpful. Thank you Spike, Jonathan, Robin, Yuval, and Stuart.

Everyone mentioned so far in this list of thanks is of the male sex. But you would be seriously mistaken if you thought that it is only to blokes that I am indebted in the writing of this book. For I live with five women: my spouse Annette, and our four daughters, Hannah, Claire, Aurora, and Emma. Of all the people in the world, and far more than any book or conference, these are the people who have taught me the most about magic. Beauty, love, goodness, wonder: I have learnt about these from you, dear hearts. Many thanks!

TEXTS CITED

Ayer, A. J. *Language, Truth and Logic*. London: Pelican, 1971.

Banks, Robert. *And Man Created God*. Oxford: Lion, 2011.

Berger, Peter L., and Thomas Luckmann. *The Social Construction of Reality*. New York: Anchor, 1967.

Chalmers, Alan. *What Is This Thing Called Science?* London: Open University Press, 2013.

Collingwood, Robin G. *An Autobiography*. London: Pelican, 1944.

Davies, Paul. *The Mind of God*. London: Penguin, 1993.

Desmond, William. *The Intimate Strangeness of Being*. Washington, DC: Catholic University of America Press, 2012.

Dupré, Louis. *Passage to Modernity*. New Haven: Yale University Press, 1993.

Franklin, James. *Corrupting the Youth. A History of Philosophy in Australia*. Sydney: Macleay, 2003.

Gardiner, Patrick. *Kierkegaard. A Very Short Introduction*. Oxford: Oxford University Press, 2002.

Gerson, Lloyd P. *Ancient Epistemology*. Cambridge: Cambridge University Press, 2009.

Gerth, Hans H., and C. Wright Mills, eds. *From Max Weber: Essays in Sociology*. London: Routledge, 1948.

Girard, René. *Violence and the Sacred*. Baltimore: John Hopkins University Press, 1979.

Harrison, Peter. *The Territories of Science and Religion*. Chicago: University of Chicago Press, 2015.

Hart, David B. *The Experience of God*. New Haven: Yale University Press, 2013.

Howland, Jacob. *The Republic. The Odyssey of Philosophy*. Philadelphia: Paul Dry, 2004.

Haynes, Kenneth, ed. *Hamann. Writings on Philosophy and Language*. Cambridge: Cambridge University Press, 2007.

Hume, David. *Dialogue concerning Natural Religion*. London: Penguin, 1990.

Josephson-Storm, Jason. *The Myth of Disenchantment*. Chicago: University of Chicago Press, 2017.

Kierkegaard, Søren. *Concluding Unscientific Postscript to the Philosophical Fragments*. Princeton: Princeton University Press, 1992.

Latour, Bruno. *We Have Never Been Modern*. Cambridge: Harvard University Press, 1993.

Numbers, Ronald L., ed. *Galileo Goes to Jail and Other Myths about Science and Religion*. Cambridge: Harvard University Press, 2009.

Oliver, Simon. *Creation: A Guide for the Perplexed*. Bloomsbury: London, 2017.

Osborne, Catherine. *Eros Unveiled*. Oxford: Clarendon, 2002.

Pasnau, Robert. *After Certainty: A History of Our Epistemic Ideals and Illusions*. Oxford: Oxford University Press, 2017.

———. *Metaphysical Themes 1274–1671*. Oxford: Oxford University Press, 2011.

Polanyi, Michael. *Personal Knowledge*. Chicago: University of Chicago Press, 1958.

———. *The Tacit Dimension*. Chicago: University of Chicago Press, 1966.

Ricoeur, Paul. *The Symbolism of Evil*. Boston: Beacon, 1992.

Ross, Chanon. *Gifts Glittering and Poisoned: Spectacle, Empire, and Metaphysics*. Eugene, OR: Cascade, 2014.

Rovelli, Carlo. *Seven Brief Lessons on Physics*. London: Penguin, 2014.

Schindler, David C. *Plato's Critique of Impure Reason*. Washington, DC: Catholic University of America Press, 2008.

Simpson, Christopher B. *The Truth Is the Way*. Veritas. Eugene, OR: Cascade, 2011.

Taylor, Charles. *A Secular Age*. Cambridge: Harvard University Press, 2007.

Made in the USA
Las Vegas, NV
30 June 2021